Discover the AWESOME WORLD

Contributors:

Camilla de la Bedoyere

John Farndon

Ian Graham

Richard Platt

Philip Steele

Miles Kelly

First published in 2012
by Miles Kelly Publishing Ltd
Harding's Barn, Bardfield End Green,
Thaxted, Essex, CM6 3PX, UK

10 9 8 7 6 5 4 3 2 1

Publishing Director Belinda Gallagher
Creative Director Jo Cowan

Managing Editors Amanda Askew, Rosie McGuire
Proofreaders Carly Blake, Claire Philip
Editorial Assistant Amy Johnson

Managing Designer Simon Lee
Design Simon Lee, D&A Design,
        Rocket Design (East Anglia) Ltd
Cover Designer Simon Lee

Production Manager Elizabeth Collins
Image Manager Liberty Newton
Reprographics Stephan Davis

ISBN 978-1-84810-855-4

Printed in China

British Library Cataloguing-in-Publication Data
A catalogue record for this book is available
from the British Library

Made with paper from a sustainable forest

www.mileskelly.net
info@mileskelly.net

www.factsforprojects.com

CONTENTS

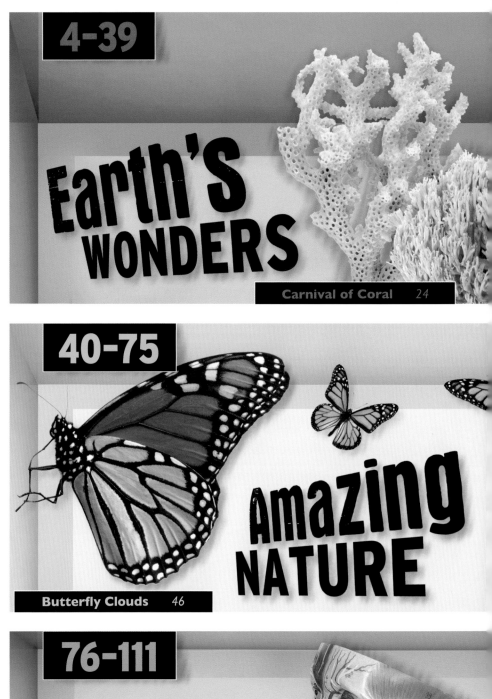

Earth's WONDERS

Embark on a whirlwind global tour and be inspired by the majesty of Earth's extraordinary natural features.

◀ On average, 38,500 cu ft (2,000 cu m) of water flows over the Victoria Falls every second, creating a mighty roar that can be heard up to 25 mi (40 km) away.

Mighty Monolith

Uluru rises majestically above a flat desert horizon in central Australia. Also known as Ayers Rock, this giant red monolith creates such an awesome spectacle—especially at dawn and dusk—that it is central to the religious faith of the indigenous people.

Island mountain

Uluru is the tip of a massive rock slab that is buried to a depth of 4 mi (6 km). Its complex history began 900 million years ago when sediments began collecting in a depression in Earth's crust. Now it is one of the last witnesses to some mammoth geological processes, including the weathering and erosion that have removed the surrounding rocks. These forces will, one day, also erase the mighty Uluru from the landscape.

▶ Uluru is composed of arkose, a type of sandstone rich in quartz and pink minerals called feldspars. The reddish color of the rock is heightened by iron oxides.

Sacred site

The local indigenous Aborigines (the Anangu) are the Traditional Owners of Uluru. They hold the area as sacred and caves at the rock's base are decorated with carvings and paintings that form part of a faith system for one of the oldest human societies in the world.

▶ Indigenous art uses symbols such as concentric circles, and animals such as kangaroos that share the land. It is used in ceremonies and storytelling.

FORMATION OF ULURU

Long ago, mountains were eroded and produced deep layers of sediment. Around 500 million years ago these sediments were drowned by a sea, covered with more sediments, and compressed to become arkose. By 300 million years ago, the arkose had been tilted upwards. Since then, the softer surrounding rocks have been eroded.

- Arkose (a type of sandstone)
- Proterozoic sedimentary rocks
- Igneous and metamorphic rocks
- Paleozoic rocks

Rectangle indicates position of Uluru over time

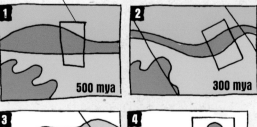

1 500 mya
2 300 mya
3 65 mya
4 Present

SUN SPECTACULAR

Uluru is known for its astonishing beauty at sunrise and sunset, when the rock takes on a luminous orange glow. As the Sun's rays pass through the atmosphere, they are filtered by dust, ash, and water vapor, especially when the Sun is low in the sky. Blue light rays are blocked, leaving the red end of the light spectrum to illuminate the rock. Uluru's natural red tones intensify the phenomenon.

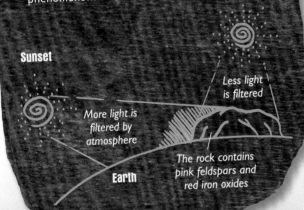

12 noon

Sunset

Less light is filtered

More light is filtered by atmosphere

The rock contains pink feldspars and red iron oxides

Earth

Many Heads

About 20 mi (32 km) west of Uluru lie 36 steep-sided rock domes. Their Aboriginal name—Kata Tjuta—describes the peaks as "Many Heads." Formed at the same time as Uluru, they are also revered as sacred sites. The largest rock, Mount Olga, gives Kata Tjuta their alternative name—The Olgas.

▼ The resistant rock of Kata Tjuta contains gravel, pebbles, and boulders all held together by a natural cement.

THE DEEP LINES THAT SCORE ULURU'S SURFACE ARE CAUSED BY WIND AND RAIN, WHICH ARE GRADUALLY WEARING AWAY THE ROCK.

Big rock at Burringurrah

Also known as Mount Augustus, Burringurrah is twice the size of Uluru, and much older. This solitary peak is one of the largest rocks in the world with a height of 2,400 ft (around 720 m). It stretches for 5 mi (8 km) and natural springs at its base have long supported the Wadjari Aboriginal people.

▼ The scrubland and waterholes around Burringurrah create a wildlife paradise where gum trees, wildflowers, reptiles, bustards, and even emus thrive.

ROCK
and Awe

The Grand Canyon is a scar on the face of Earth that is visible from space. This long, wide, and very deep chasm is a slice through our planet's mind-boggling history—and it is still growing.

▼ Viewed by satellite, the mighty Colorado River looks like a meandering stream within the snow-covered chasm that surrounds it.

Rainbow rocks

The Grand Canyon forms part of an incredible vista at any time of day, but as the Sun settles behind the distant horizon its fabulous colors become even more evident. Pale pinks and lilacs give way to brilliant reds and neon oranges while the sky becomes an inky wash. Golden light and deep shadows emphasize the canyon's countless ridges, pinnacles, and valleys, highlighting the colossal scale of this breathtaking panorama.

Howdy hoodoo

It's hard to imagine that bizarre amphitheaters of rock populated by needlelike pinnacles (hoodoos) were once vast plateaus of solid rock that have been sculpted by erosion and the weather. Bryce Canyon (below) was named after a pioneer who built a ranch there in the 1870s and remarked that it was a terrible place to lose a cow!

▼ The tallest pinnacle at Bryce Canyon is called Thor's Hammer and is a popular spot for tourists viewing a spectacular sunset.

▲ The view from Toroweap Outlook takes in the Inner Canyon and its heart—the Colorado River.

THE GRAND CANYON COVERS FOUR ERAS OF GEOLOGICAL TIME, FIVE HABITATS, AND FOUR DESERT TYPES, AS WELL AS UNIQUE FOSSIL AND ARCHEOLOGICAL RECORDS.

◄ Californian condors are one of the largest bird species in North America, with a wingspan of 9 ft (around 3 m). They are also one of the world's rarest birds.

Welcome home

For millions of years, Californian condors have soared over the canyon. They search for carcasses to feed on, making the most of thermal air currents that help them glide effortlessly over long distances. A range of threats, including poisoning and habitat loss, saw their numbers plummet to just 22 individuals in 1982. The condor remains an endangered species but a captive breeding program, and reintroductions to the wild, have resulted in condors once again flying above the canyon.

ELECTRIC DISPLAY

A summer's evening at the canyon can become a spectacle of flashing light and rumbling thunder, as storms brew and electrical charges build in the intense heat. Lightning strikes somewhere in the canyon around 26,000 times a year, and each bolt may split dramatically in the sky, forking toward the ground and striking points up to 5 mi (8 km) apart. It usually hits areas of high elevation, especially scorched skeleton trees that line the rim. Dead and scorched skeleton trees around the canyon's highest edges bear testament to nature's grim power.

A slice in time

The Colorado River, which carved the canyon, is almost out of sight as it continues its ancient path through the rocks. As it flows, the river has sculpted a deep chasm through layers of sedimentary rocks, exposing bands of color. The top layers are just 260 million years old, while at the bottom, the river has reached rocks that are one mile (1.6 km) down and almost ten times older.

SYMPHONY
of Spectacles

People have been shaping their habitats for millennia, and nowhere is this more evident than Rio de Janeiro, Brazil. Situated in one of the most spectacular landscapes on Earth, this is a bustling modern city where nature's beauty provides the awe, and sweeping urbanization packs the punch.

Peachy beaches

Tourists throng Rio's world-famous coast, enjoying the sunshine and sea along the magnificent 2.5 mi (4 km) crescent of white sand that is Copacabana Beach. Here, waterfront hotels, shops, and restaurants are as much part of the scenery as the backdrop of forest-covered hills.

▼ Citizens of Rio, or *Cariocas*, flock to Copacabana Beach in the day to play, swim, and laze in the sunshine, but in the evening, partying takes over.

◀ Sugarloaf Mountain is 1,299 ft (396 m) tall and juts into the sky at the tip of the bay's peninsula.

Landmark peak

Rio is generally agreed to be one of the most stunning harbor cities in the world. Built on a series of hills, Brazil's carnival city is still flanked by swathes of virgin forest and enjoys a stunning view over Guanabara Bay and granite islands. Sugarloaf Mountain, however, has long been the area's iconic feature and is still an ideal landmark for sailors approaching Rio after an arduous journey across the Atlantic.

CABLE CARS HAVE FERRIED ABOUT 37 MILLION VISITORS TO SUGARLOAF SINCE 1912. THEY ENJOY THE JOURNEY OF A LIFETIME AND PANORAMIC VIEWS OF RIO AND ITS BAY.

Rocky Corcovado

Corcovado is a huge granite peak named after the Portuguese word for "hunchback." Both Sugarloaf and Corcovado are volcanic formations that were once underground. Over hundreds of millions of years, the softer rock on top wore away, leaving these strange rocks exposed as steep-sided mountains—so steep that soil cannot form so they remain bare rock. Where the sea has flooded into the gaps between the granite islands as sea levels rose, beautiful curving bays are created.

BRAZIL · RIO DE JANEIRO · RIO DE JANEIRO · BRAZIL

▲ Tourists visiting Christ the Redeemer have the best views over the city and bay. The statue was built in the Art Deco style and completed in 1931.

CRADLE of Life

One of the most striking natural wonders of the world, the Great Rift Valley extends from Jordan to Mozambique. This enormous system of valleys, lakes, plateaus, mountains, and volcanoes is home to millions of animals and contains Olduvai Gorge, an area of Tanzania regarded as the cradle of human life.

AFRICA

SHIFT AND SHAKE

The Great Rift Valley is the ever-widening gap between two vast tectonic plates that are moving gradually apart. Starting in southwestern Asia, this dramatic steep-sided valley cuts through East Africa, completely dividing every country it passes through. The valley and its landforms extend for 4,000 mi (around 6,500 km) and are also known as the East African Rift System. Already in the north, the sea has flooded in to form the Red Sea—and eventually East Africa will separate from the rest and the Rift Valley will be an ocean.

▼ The grasslands of the Ngorongoro Crater are home for many Maasai people, who practice nomadic pastoralism.

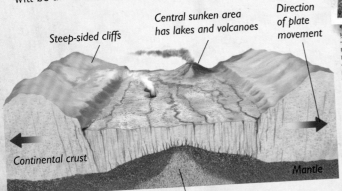

Steep-sided cliffs

Central sunken area has lakes and volcanoes

Direction of plate movement

Continental crust

Mantle

Magma plume

▲ Upwelling heat in Earth's mantle forces plates apart and causes plenty of volcanic activity along the valley floor. As the plates move, brittle rock is put under enormous pressure and breaks along fault lines.

Ngorongoro Crater

In the southern region of the Great Rift Valley lies the Ngorongoro Crater, the remains of an extinct, collapsed volcano. At up to 14 mi (22.5 km) across and 2,000 ft (610 m) deep, it is the world's largest complete and unflooded caldera (collapsed volcanic crater). Its steep sides help to create the crater's own weather system, and within its "walls" a unique ecosystem exists. The wildlife here is largely isolated from bigger populations that live beyond the Ngorongoro.

Kilimanjaro's tallest peak reaches 19,340 ft (5,895 m) and is the highest point in Africa.

EGYPT

RED SEA

ERITREA

SUDAN

DJIBOUTI

ETHIOPIA

SOMALIA

East African Rift Zone

UGANDA

KENYA

Lake Victoria

Ngorongoro Crater

Mount Kilimanjaro

Lake Tanganyika

DEMOCRATIC REPUBLIC OF THE CONGO

TANZANIA

Lake Malawi

MALAWI

MOZAMBIQUE

ZAMBIA

Peak icing

A volcanic massif (group of mountains), Kilimanjaro is formed mostly from three large extinct volcanoes. The youngest volcanic cone, Kibo, retains an ice cap all year but global warming and deforestation are having a dramatic impact on the massif's iconic icing, which may soon disappear.

The remains of the first tool-using human ancestor, Homo habilis, and early man, Paranthropus bosei, are some of the anthropological treasures discovered at Olduvai Gorge in the Rift System, leading scientists to believe that human evolution began in this region.

▼ Lake Malawi provides a range of habitats for wildlife, from deep clear water to sandy beaches and wooded hillsides.

Great Lakes

The western branch of the Rift System hosts the African Great Lakes, where the rift filled with water. Lake Malawi is known for its great size, the clarity of its water, and the astonishing biodiversity it supports—it contains the largest number of fish species of any lake in the world. Lake Victoria is Africa's largest lake by area and is the source of the White Nile. Long, slender Lake Tanganyika is the second deepest lake in the world.

Wild **Wetland**

The Pantanal is the largest-known freshwater wetland in the world, and it is a paradise for animals and plants. It extends from Brazil into Paraguay and Bolivia, covering at least 50,000 sq mi (129,500 sq km)—an area bigger than 29 of the U.S. states.

Seasonal soakings

An immense low-lying floodplain, the Pantanal contains some areas that are permanently swamped wildernesses. During the seasonal soakings, when rains in the nearby highlands pour into the river systems, the rivers burst their banks and the area underwater increases to around 80 percent.

Super habitat

Seasonal flooding sees a peak in fish breeding in the swampy plains, but during the dry season, from May to September, large areas of land are exposed and dry out. Grazing animals move in, closely followed by their predators—jaguars. Wading birds feast on the fish left exposed in isolated pools and a diverse range of animals feed among giant lily pads and water hyacinths.

▼ There are at least 50 species of reptile in the Pantanal. Yellow anacondas give birth to their young in water.

▼ Spectacled caimans are the most adaptable of all crocodilians, so they can tolerate the Pantanal's changing conditions.

▼ Floodwaters on the Pantanal can reach 13 ft (4 m) in height during and after the long summer rainy season, creating challenging conditions for cowboys and their herds.

Alien invaders

Cattle have been grazing on the Pantanal for around 260 years and many millions are now kept on enormous ranches. Large areas of woody vegetation have been removed using the cut-and-slash method, or by burning, to produce more grazing land.

▲ An incredible array of wildlife lives on the Pantanal, including the world's largest rodents, capybaras, which have a body length of about 3.3 ft (1 m). They are adept swimmers.

Adios Pantanal?

The Pantanal has been described as "one of the last intact ecological paradises." However, cattle ranching, commercial hunting, and pollution are just a few of the growing threats to this habitat. While some recent large-scale plans to turn the Paraguay River into a more navigable route for cargo have been put on hold, other projects planned for the rivers and tributaries that feed the wetlands are still being developed. This is likely to increase the environmental pressures that already face this precious ecosystem.

"PANTANAL" MEANS "SWAMP," BUT ACTUALLY THE REGION IS A PLAIN, AND THE REMAINS OF AN ANCIENT INLAND SEA THAT IS SLOWLY DRYING OUT.

WHITE Out

The astonishing all-white vista created by a large salt flat makes for a formidable sight. These dried-out lakes are some of Earth's flattest surfaces, and the salt crystals that cover them reflect the Sun's rays to create glimmering, shimmering spectacles.

All dried up

Salar de Uyuni is a huge windswept salt flat high on Bolivia's Altiplano (high plain). It is found at an elevation of 11,995 ft (3,656 m) above sea level and covers an area of 4,085 sq mi (10,580 sq km). Beneath several feet of salt lies a salty pool of water that belonged, around 40,000 years ago, to a much larger body of water—the prehistoric Lake Minchin. Over time, heat has evaporated the water, allowing salt to precipitate out as a solid. Salar de Uyuni receives seasonal flooding, and when covered in a thin film of water it creates one of the world's largest natural mirrors.

Pass the salt

The high concentration of salt in these lakes creates an inhospitable environment, although a few species manage to survive. Salar de Uyuni also supports human life in the form of mining communities and tourism. The mined salt is used in building materials. In the future, mining may concentrate on extracting vast reserves of lithium, which lies beneath the salt-encrusted surface. This soft metal is used primarily by ceramics and glass industries, and in the production of batteries.

◄ Giant cacti grow on Inkahuasi Island, a rocky outcrop in Salar de Uyuni. They have a dense covering of spines, which are modified leaves, and flower periodically.

▲ Salt is shoveled into small piles, then transported by truck.

Tiny islands

While the salt plain is almost perfectly flat, there are protrusions that rise above its pristine white surface. These rocky outcrops near the middle of the lake are the remnants of volcanoes that existed on the plain before being flooded by the ancient Lake Minchin. They contain fossils that provide evidence of this region's submerged history, and today they provide an oasis in the sea of vast, blinding whiteness. On these islands hardy animals and plants can survive, including cacti. When the lake is flooded, South American flamingos also visit, to feed and breed.

◄ As the Sun slides toward the horizon, the sheets of white salt take on a stunning blue hue, and rock islands create strange shadows.

SALAR DE UYUNI IS THE WORLD'S LARGEST SALT FLAT, AND THE DIFFERENCE FROM ITS LOWEST PARTS TO ITS HIGHEST PARTS IS NO GREATER THAN 3 FT (80 CM).

TRAIN CEMETERY
Old train tracks connect the lake to the nearby town of Uyuni. Cargoes of salt were taken from the lake to the town by train, and onward to ports. The locomotives are no longer used, but have been left to decay in an area known as the "train cemetery."

DRAGON'S Jewels

At Halong Bay, on the border of Vietnam and China, geology and mythology combine to create a mysterious seascape of limestone pillars, islands, and islets. It was once believed that these strange rocky outcrops were placed there by dragons to defend the land from invasion.

Drowned rocks

During Earth's history the sea level has risen and fallen after the planet's climate has undergone large changes. When seawater is trapped in ice the sea level falls; when global warming occurs the ice melts, and the sea level rises. It was this process that caused the sea to invade a karst (limestone) mountain landscape on the Vietnamese coast, in an area now called the Gulf of Tonkin, and create Halong Bay. The strange shape of the islands comes from the way that limestone is dissolved by acidic rainwater. Today, the bay contains more than 2,000 islands, each covered with virgin jungles. They are still largely uninhabited and unspoilt.

▼ The water in Halong Bay is mostly less than 30 ft (around 10 m) deep, and covers a drowned karst plain.

▼ As acid rain erodes the islands they can develop into unusual shapes, giving rise to their local names, such as "Elephant" and "Wallowing Buffalo."

Jade and jewels

According to ancient legend, Halong Bay was formed when the region was under invasion, and dragons came to defend the land. As they descended from the sky, the dragons spat out thousands of pearls. Each pearl hit the water and turned into a jade island, and together the islands created an impenetrable barrier to the invading ships.

Caves of awe

Marine erosion has continued to shape and form the landscape, carving out many more caves and grottoes, adding to those created before the coast was flooded. Hang Sung Sot ("Cave of Awe"), for example, is one of the oldest caves in the area and has passages that are more than 33 ft (10 m) high and wide that lead downward to caves filled with stalagmites and boulders.

THE TOWERS OF LIMESTONE HAVE NEAR-VERTICAL SIDES. ROCKFALLS ARE COMMON AND HUGE SLABS OF ROCK OFTEN PEEL OFF AND SLAM INTO THE SEA BELOW.

THE INVADING SEA

Rain falling on limestone creates acid, which dissolves the rock and creates tunnels, caves, and shafts called sinkholes. When the sea invades, this "drowned karst" landscape is the result.

Older caves formed when the sea level was higher

Hills

Chasm

Tower

Recently formed cave

Drowned chasm

PinNaCLEs
and Pillars

When the world's weathering processes get to work, the landscape can be utterly transformed. Changes in air temperature, and moisture and chemicals in the atmosphere, can carve strange pillars, columns, and pinnacles from solid stone, producing a spectacular range of scenery.

▼ Parts of Cappadocia's bizarre landscape are protected within the boundaries of the Goreme National Park in Turkey.

Fairy chimneys

In Turkey's Cappadocia region, thousands of conical structures appear to rise out of the ground, reaching up to 165 ft (50 m) in height. These are the remains of a vast blanket of volcanic ash that solidified into a soft rock called tuff. Over millions of years, erosion has removed much of the tuff and sculpted these towers, which are known as fairy chimneys. More resistant rock forms mushroomlike caps on some of them.

Twelve Apostles

Coastal rock stacks are witnesses to the immense ability of the sea to carve solid rock. The Twelve Apostles in Australia are limestone stacks that stand along a high-energy coast. They were once part of a large limestone bed that has been slowly demolished by wind, waves, and rain. They continue to disappear at a rate of one inch (2.5 cm) a year.

▲ Australia's Twelve Apostles were originally known as The Sow and her Pigs, before being renamed in the 1950s.

The Needles

When Lot's Wife, a 120 ft (37 m) sea stack in coastal waters by the Isle of Wight, collapsed into the sea during a storm in the 18th century, it was said that the sound could be heard miles away. Lot's Wife was tall and thin, which is why the group of sea stacks it belonged to are known as The Needles, even though the three remaining stacks are quite stumpy. A lighthouse clings to the furthermost Needle, to warn shipping of the collapsed stack below the waves.

▼ The Needles in southern England are formed of chalk, a soft, white limestone.

Moonscape on Earth

The Pinnacles Desert in Australia has a spectral quality, and it is often compared to a scene from a science fiction movie. At sunset the stone structures rise from a bed of golden sand and are set against a sky that is washed in pinks, golds, and lilacs. The Pinnacles were formed recently in geological time and they are the remains of a limestone bed that has been eroded, chemically changed by rainwater, and further altered by plants.

▲ The tallest structures in the Pinnacles Desert are 11.5 ft (3.5 m) tall.

Bald Heads

The large balancing boulders at Matobo Hills in Zimbabwe have been called Ama Tobo, or Bald Heads. They are made of granite, which formed under intense heat and pressure during a volcanic mountain-building phase. Cracks in the rock have helped the elements erode the boulders into these strange shapes. Cecil Rhodes, the founder of Rhodesia—now Zimbabwe and Zambia—is buried here.

▼ Stacks of rocks defy gravity at Matobo Hills.

Smoke that THUNDERS

As the mighty Zambezi River plunges over a vertical cliff-edge, a thunderous roar fills the chasm below. A vast, white veil of mist plumes upward, giving the Victoria Falls its local name of *Mosi-oa-Tunya*, which means "The Smoke that Thunders."

Falling sheets

The Victoria Falls is neither the tallest nor the widest waterfall, but it can lay claim to producing the largest single sheet of water in the world. In full flood, during February and March, more than 18 million cu ft (500,000 cu m) of water cascades over the precipice every second. Sited at the border of Zambia and Zimbabwe, the falls span nearly 6,000 ft (1,800 m) at the widest point, and have a maximum drop of 355 ft (108 m).

▼ The Victoria Falls cascades over the lip of a large rocky plateau. The mass of water has been slicing slowly through this rock for two million years.

Gouging gorges

After the water pummels the rocks at the bottom of the Victoria Falls, it continues its journey through a narrow zigzag series of gorges, passing seven points where the falls were once sited. Water erosion continues to gouge out weaker areas in a vast plateau of basalt rock, moving the falls further and further up the river's course.

▶ After descending the falls, the wide Zambezi is forced through a long zigzag series of extremely narrow chasms, increasing the speed and force of the water's flow.

Devil's Pool

Tourists flock to the Victoria Falls and, when the river levels drop, those looking for an adrenaline rush can enjoy the surreal—and risky—experience of bathing on a cliff edge. The Devil's Pool has a natural rock wall that (in theory) prevents swimmers from being dragged over the top by the raging water's momentum.

▲ Low water levels between September and December allow tourists to enter the Devil's Pool and swim perilously close to the falls' edge.

THE VICTORIA FALLS IS ABOUT TWICE AS WIDE AND DEEP AS THE NIAGARA FALLS. ITS SHIMMERING MIST CAN BE SEEN MORE THAN 12 MI (20 KM) AWAY.

Angel Falls

The best way to appreciate the awesome spectacle of the world's tallest falls is by air. In fact, the Angel Falls in Venezuela was named after U.S. pilot Jimmy Angel, who got a bird's-eye view when he crash-landed nearby in 1937. The Churún River gushes over the Angel Falls at such a rate that water scarcely touches the cliff face as it plummets 3,212 ft (979 m).

▲ In Venezuela the Angel Falls is known as *Kerepakupai Merú*, which means "waterfall of the deepest place."

23

CARNIVAL
of Coral

The enormous size of the Great Barrier Reef needs a long-distance view because its thousands of individual reefs and islands stretch for over 1,240 mi (2,000 km). Getting to grips with its astounding impact on nature, however, means going underwater.

▼ The reef is made up of 3,000 smaller reefs and 1,000 islands.

Slow-grow

A reef is a slow-growing structure of rocky carbonate compounds and the living coral polyps that create them. Australia's Great Barrier Reef is the planet's most extensive coral-reef system and one of the largest structures ever made by living things. The reef has been growing for 18 million years. The living parts, which are growing on top of the older sections, began forming after the last Ice Age, 8,000–20,000 years ago.

1. *Planula searches for a place to settle*

▼ *Polyps can reproduce in two ways. An egg can grow into a planula, or an adult can make a bud, which grows into a twin of itself.*

4. *Coral colony begins to grow through "budding"*

3. *Polyp begins to grow a stony cup*

2. *Planula attaches to a hard surface*

▲ Yonge Reef is a popular part of the Great Barrier Reef for divers because of the huge diversity of its corals and other wildlife.

Critical critters

Coral polyps are soft-bodied animals related to sea anemones. They live in extensive colonies and secrete minerals to create protective cups around themselves. It is these cups that make up the bulk of a reef structure. Corals that grow near the surface in sunlit waters have a symbiotic relationship with zooxanthellae algae. The corals provide the algae with carbon dioxide, nutrients, and a safe place to live; the algae give the corals sugar and oxygen from photosynthesis.

THE SINGLE BIGGEST THREAT TO CORAL REEFS IS THOUGHT TO BE POLLUTION, BUT THIS FRAGILE ECOSYSTEM IS EASILY DAMAGED AND IS AT RISK FROM NUMEROUS FACTORS, INCLUDING TOURISM AND GLOBAL WARMING.

REEF ENCOUNTERS

Islanders from the Torres Strait and Aborigines from Australia have been fishing around the Barrier Reef for more than 60,000 years. They are now known as the Traditional Owners of the Great Barrier Reef, and work to conserve the region's biodiversity, and its cultural history. Scientists began studying the reef in the 18th century, after the ship of British explorer James Cook ran aground on the coral.

▲ Nautiluses have scarcely changed in millions of years, and are considered to be living fossils.

Rain forest of the sea

A journey under the sea reveals another magical side to the reef: in the silence of the turquoise waters an underwater carnival of colors is revealed. The reef provides a habitat for an enormous range of wildlife, producing an astonishing level of biodiversity. Schools of tiny silvery fish dart between the weirdly shaped corals, and on their rocky surfaces there are pink mollusks, blue starfish, purple anemones, transparent shrimps, and garish worms. Large predators, such as sharks and squid, venture close to shore to feed and breed. The coral provides plenty of hiding places.

◄ Sweetlips fish undergo incredible color transformations as they age, often becoming less colorful but more boldly patterned.

▼ Jellyfish are closely related to the coral polyps that build the reef. They move with a pulsing rhythm and catch animals in their stinging tentacles.

Valley of THE MOON

Captivatingly beautiful in its austerity, Wadi Rum has inspired many writers to attempt to describe the maze of skyscraper-like monoliths that rise from the desert sand. Part of this landscape's spectacular impact comes from the play of light on the rocks, and the life-giving effect of water in an arid land.

Vast valleys

The Wadi Rum valley cuts through south Jordan. Layers of beige, orange, red, and gray sedimentary sandstones rest upon an ancient layer of granite that is more than 2,000 million years old. The tectonic events that continue to shape the Great Rift Valley have tilted and fractured the sandstones, which have been eroded by wind and rain into stone sculptures, arches, and canyons.

▼ One of the rock formations in Wadi Rum was named after T. E. Lawrence's book *The Seven Pillars of Wisdom*—although the seven pillars in the book have no connection with Wadi Rum.

◀▼ Desert scenes in the 1962 movie, *Lawrence of Arabia*, were shot in Wadi Rum, which was the original location of much of the historical action.

Lawrence of Arabia

Wadi Rum was an important site during World War I (1914–1918) when the Arabs were in revolt against the Ottomans. Prince Faisal Bin Hussein and British soldier T. E. Lawrence (known as Lawrence of Arabia) made their base here.

COLUMBIA PICTURES presents THE SAM SPIEGEL · DAVID LEAN Production of

LAWRENCE OF ARABIA

WINNER OF
7 ACADEMY AWARDS

STARRING
ALEC GUINNESS · ANTHONY QUINN · JACK HAWKINS · JOS
ANTHONY QUAYLE · CLAUDE RAINS · ARTHUR KENNEDY
WITH OMAR SHARIF as 'ALI' introducing and PETER O'TOOLE as 'LA..RENCE'
A HORIZON BRITISH PRODUCTION IN TECHNICOLOR

Spring awakening

After the winter rains, Wadi Rum's natural springs swell, causing the desert to explode with life. Plants such as poppies and black irises bloom in the usually barren ground, and hardy animals such as snakes, ibex, gray wolves, and foxes also survive in the harsh landscape.

▼ The desert lark is one of more than 100 bird species that have been recorded at Wadi Rum.

▶ Crocuses rest as corms during dry periods, but grow and flower after rainfall.

A POPULAR MOVIE LOCATION, WADI RUM WAS USED TO PORTRAY THE SURFACE OF MARS IN "RED PLANET" (2000) AND EGYPT IN "TRANSFORMERS: REVENGE OF THE FALLEN" (2009).

▼ The tectonic events that continue to shape the Rift Valley have tilted and fractured the sandstones of Wadi Rum. They have been eroded by wind, rain, and flash floods into red cliffs and deep canyons.

▼ Jordan's Desert Patrol still sends its famous Camel Corps to police areas of the Wadi Rum where even Land Rovers cannot reach.

Intrepid travelers

People have been traveling through this desert for millennia. Many of them have left archeological evidence that hints at the region's rich history, from flint axes and prehistoric rock carvings to the remains of a 2,000-year-old temple built by Nabataean people. Today, tribal Bedouins still herd their goats through the canyons, camping in goat-hair tents when following their traditional nomadic lifestyle.

ICE
Mountains

In Europe, the Alps form a vast mountain barrier. They dominate the continent, shaping its land and even affecting its culture and history. Although they are situated in a temperate region, the Alps endure lashing ice storms in winter and the peaks stay snowy all year round.

Pyramid peak

With its steep, angular peak the Matterhorn is Europe's iconic mountain—easy to recognize and with a dangerous reputation. Despite its height, the Matterhorn's four faces are virtually snowless because of their steepness. The first ascent of the mountain took place in 1865, with a loss of four lives. Since then, many hundreds more climbers have died scaling its heights, and the Matterhorn still has one of the highest death rates in the world.

▲ The Matterhorn straddles the border between Switzerland and Italy and is 14,693 ft (4,478 m) tall. Italians call it *Monte Cervino*. It requires great technical skill to climb because the rock is unstable, and variable weather conditions prevail.

▼ As the glacier grinds onward, the combination of the great weight of ice and the rocks inside it scours the landscape.

Making mountains

The Alps are 650 mi (about 1,050 km) long and up to 120 mi (about 200 km) wide. Several Alpine mountains are more than 13,000 ft (4,000 m) tall, and the tallest is Mont Blanc in France. The range began to form about 90 million years ago when two tectonic plates began to converge. The plates crushed and folded the layers of rock between them, forcing them into mountains and valleys, which have been eroded and shaped by glaciation in the last two million years.

Great glaciers

The Aletsch Glacier is an enormous frozen river of ice moving slowly southward from Alpine peaks toward the Rhône Valley. Although it is moving downhill because of gravity, the glacier's front is retreating because it melts as it comes down into warmer air. Water flowing under the ice causes the glacier to deposit its cargo of rocks, creating sediments known as moraines. The Aletsch is Europe's largest valley glacier, measuring 16 mi (25 km), although it has retreated about 2 mi (3 km) in the last 150 years.

▼ The flowers in an Alpine meadow are usually small and low-growing to minimize damage from winds and frosts. They help to create stunning summer panoramas, with backdrops of snow-tipped mountains.

Alpine meadows

Even mighty mountains are not strong enough to withstand the weather. Over millions of years rain, ice, wind, and snow eroded the Alpine rocks, gradually turning them, with organic debris, into soil that can support meadows. The high Alpine meadows are relatively inaccessible, and are now some of Europe's least spoilt habitats. Seemingly fragile plants can survive under snow during winter, then burst into life when the snow melts, creating a dazzling carpet of flowers.

WILDLIFE
Hideaway

The island of Madagascar is a place like no other—literally. It broke away from Africa 150–180 million years ago and now exists as a mini-continent of natural wonders with a bewilderingly diverse range of landscapes and wildlife.

MASSIVE MASSIF

An enormous sheer rock face draws adventurers to central Madagascar. Known as the Tsaranoro Massif, the 2,600-ft (800-m) granite cliff is almost vertical, making it an interesting challenge for climbers, and an awesome spot for the bravest paragliders and base jumpers.

▲ With nowhere to camp out, climbers aim to climb the granite cliffs of Tsaranoro in just one day. The rock faces are solid without cracks, so climbers drill bolts into the cliff to ascend new routes.

MAD

SPLITTING UP

At 226,662 sq mi (587,051 sq km) in area, Madagascar is Earth's fourth largest island but it was once part of a giant landmass called Gondwana. Around 180 million years ago a chunk of eastern Gondwana began to move away from Africa. More separations followed, forming Antarctica, India, Australia, and Madagascar.

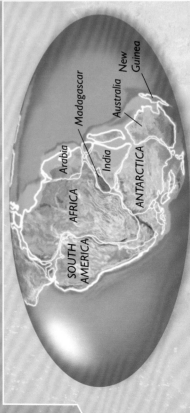

▲ Gondwana was one of two supercontinents that would eventually split into smaller landmasses. It contained most of the landmasses that are in today's Southern Hemisphere, including Madagascar (red).

SOUTH AMERICA
AFRICA
Arabia
India
Madagascar
Australia
New Guinea
ANTARCTICA

TREASURE TROVES

Separated from the rest of the world, Madagascar embarked on its own evolutionary journey, and most of the species of animals and plants found here live nowhere else. Although much of Madagascar's rain forest has been felled, the remaining areas still harbor 8,000 species of endemic plants, more than 1,000 types of spider, and about 300 species of frog.

▶ Watery habitats are home to many amphibians and fish.

LEMURS ALL ALONE

The first mammals arrived about 60 million years ago, long after the island had been formed. It is thought they arrived on rafts of floating vegetation, and their evolutionary progress continued down a different path to those they had left behind. About 40 species of lemurs, a type of primate with large eyes and foxlike faces, evolved here.

▲ Brown lemurs rarely leave the forest canopy, and feed on fruit, leaves, tree sap, and bugs.

TSINGY LANDS

Parts of Madagascar are virtually impenetrable, where razor-sharp pyramids of rock emerge from the ground. The rocks are so closely packed together it is difficult to find a path between them. They are known as "tsingy" locally, because they make a bell-like sound when struck.

▶ The tsingy peaks were molded by the chemical reaction between rainwater and limestone.

UPSIDE-DOWN TREES

Peculiar baobabs are the iconic trees of the island. Their swollen trunks hold huge stores of water to help the plants get through the dry season, and some baobabs have lived for more than 1,000 years. Lemurs and giant moths suck nectar from their flowers. There are eight species of baobab, and six of them live only on Madagascar.

▶ The Avenue of the Baobabs was once surrounded by lush forest.

frozen Kingdom

Carved by glaciers and exposed to some of Earth's most menacing weather, Svalbard is home to one of the planet's last great wildernesses. This collection of islands lies inside the Arctic Circle and encounters extraordinary phenomena, including the Northern Lights.

▲ Aurorae occur at heights of 50–600 mi (80–1000 km) above Earth, and these silent, flickering displays can be any combination of green, yellow, blue, and red.

Glacier on the move

About 80 percent of Spitsbergen, the main island in Svalbard, is covered by glaciers. One of the most famous of these is Kongsvegen. This mighty river of ice covers about 40 sq mi (105 sq km) and has a length of about 12 mi (20 km). As its low-lying tip, or terminus, reaches the sea, enormous chunks of ice break off to form icebergs.

▲ As Kongsvegen reaches the sea it extends into the Kongsfjorden (a fjord) and icebergs (in the foreground) break away.

▲ The molecular structure of ice is less dense than that of liquid water. This means that icebergs can float in seas and rivers.

Archipelago of ice

Spitsbergen's snowcapped Tre-Kroner Mountains give way to a huge inlet called Kongsfjorden, where ice-cold Arctic waters meet the warmer Atlantic Ocean. Enormous icebergs litter the entrance of the fjord, but the warmer waters entice an unexpected array of wildlife to the area, from fulmars to black-legged kittiwakes. In summer, up to three million birds flock to Svalbard, where they are able to feed for 24 hours when the midnight Sun lights up the land, even during the dead of night.

Northern Lights

Under a still, cold winter's sky, one of the most extraordinary reminders of the planet's place in a bigger Universe is often on view. The Northern Lights, or *Aurora Borealis*, are fleeting visible displays of electrical and magnetic forces. Sheets of light move across the star-studded sky, and their sweeping spectral colors indicate that electric particles from solar winds are splitting oxygen and nitrogen-based molecules in the atmosphere.

IN 1925 EXPLORER ROALD AMUNDSEN ATTEMPTED TO FLY FROM SVALBARD TO THE NORTH POLE IN A DORNIER WAL FLYING BOAT—AND FAILED.

Sparkling snowbows

When sunlight hits rain it can trigger a rainbow, and when it hits flakes of falling snow, a rare sight—the snowbow—may result. Ice crystals in snow bend, or refract, light rays causing them to separate into their constituent rainbow colors.

▶ Snowbows are rare phenomena because they only form in conditions of bright sunlight and light snow.

▼ Polar bears take what they can find. This predator is scavenging on the remains of a fin whale.

Arctic hunters

Svalbard is shared by humans and other mammals that are better equipped to withstand the extreme weather. Polar bears are one of the few mammals that will actively hunt humans, although they usually feed on seals instead. They roam over huge areas in Svalbard, and are as adept at swimming as they are at walking over vast expanses of ice.

Big Island's FIRE

Many of Earth's most awesome features and processes lie hidden beneath its surface. At volcanic hotspots, however, the majestic power of our planet is on view, and there are few better places to witness it than in Hawaii.

HAWAII'S BIG ISLAND

According to Native Hawaiian mythology, when Pele—the goddess of volcanoes—is angry she stamps her feet, causing earthquakes, and starts volcanic eruptions with a shake of her magic stick. If the myth is true, Pele must be furious with Hawaii's Big Island—this is a record-breaking volcanic hotspot without equal on Earth.

MAUNA LOA

- The world's largest active volcano.
- Dome is 64 miles (103 km) across.
- One of the biggest single mountains in the world.
- In 1950, a lava flow from a single fissure devastated a nearby village.

Aloha Mauna Loa

Mauna Loa's great mass covers more than half of Hawaii's Big Island. Its first well-documented eruption occurred in 1843 and Mauna Loa has erupted more than 30 times since. By radiocarbon-dating the lava, scientists have discovered that the first eruption occurred up to one million years ago—and it is almost certain that it will erupt again.

▼ Lava fountains on Mauna Loa spew out from fissures during an eruption. The lava is almost fluid, so it flows easily.

▼ Kea's often snow-capped dome has numerous cinder cones—deposits that build up around volcanic vents.

MAUNA KEA

- 5.6 mi (9 km) in height from its base on the ocean floor.
- Dome is 30 mi (50 km) across.
- The world's largest astronomical observatory is sited on its slopes.

Colossal Kea

The islands of Hawaii have been developing over the last five million years—the result of volcanoes forming as the Pacific tectonic plate passes over a hotspot in Earth's mantle layer. Mauna Kea, which is now dormant, began erupting on the seafloor about 800,000 years ago and if it is measured from this base Kea is actually taller than Mount Everest. Its last eruption occurred 4,500 years ago but volcanologists believe it may be spurred into action again.

◀ Aside from its enormous volcanoes, Big Island also has many climate zones, from jungles to snow-topped mountains.

FIREFIGHTERS

Volcanologists conduct crucial work, often putting their lives at risk to gather information about volcanic activity. They are still unable to accurately predict earthquakes and volcanoes, but collecting data such as changes in temperature, gases, lava flows, and seismic activity help to build accurate pictures of precursors to major tectonic events.

KILAUEA

- The world's most active volcano.
- Spews, on average, 130,000 gal (around 492,000 l) of lava every minute.
- Repeated explosive eruptions make it one of the most dangerous volcanoes on Earth.

▼ Black, burning lava from Kilauea spews into the sea, below a hardened lava crust.

Constant eruption

The sights, sounds, and smells of an active volcano smother the senses. Pungent gases, ash, and lava have been erupting from one of the cinder cones (called Pu`u Ó) of Kilauea since 1983. It may be a young shield volcano, with most of its structure still below sea level, but Kilauea has wreaked devastation on its environment, destroying ancient archeological sites, villages, and rain forest.

EMERALD Scene

In 3,000 places on Mexico's Yucatán Peninsula the Sun's warming rays pass through pools or shafts known as cenotes. These holes in the landscape are entrance points to a spectacular underworld that features flooded caverns, ancient Mayan ceremonial altars, and blind fish.

▶ Lush tropical vegetation surrounds Yucatán's cenotes, thanks to a plentiful supply of groundwater in the region.

Sun-filled basins

In Yucatán, most of these caverns contain pools of sparkling groundwater that is incredibly clean, having been filtered by its passage through the limestone. In some places, shafts of light reach down into the caverns, and plants are able to grow. Deep pools of water are home to species of blind fish, and colonies of bats roost along dark stone ledges.

◀ Belize slider turtles feed on vegetation in cenotes, but can clamber out to bask in the sunlight.

The Place of Fear

Few rivers run across the land above this subterranean structure, as all the water flows down holes and into the caverns beneath, in some instances creating cenotes. These wells had great meaning to the Mayans who lived here—they were seen as gateways to the underworld, known as *Xibalba*, or the "Place of Fear." Some cenotes were used as water sources, but others were used for the purpose of sacrifice, and people were thrown into the pools to appease the god of rain.

▲ This ancient skull was found in a cenote, and was possibly that of a human sacrifice victim.

Big impact

The surrounding rock was once part of a giant limestone plain, which was probably damaged by the Chicxulub meteorite that fell here around 65 million years ago, sparking the demise of the dinosaurs. The rock plateau has been further weakened and dissolved by rainwater. Over time, small caves and tunnels have collapsed, creating enormous caverns.

VISION IS OF NO USE TO LITTLE DAMA FISH LIVING IN DARK CENOTES, SO OVER TIME THEY HAVE LOST THEIR EYES.

Flower caves

About 300 mi (500 km) of the caves and watery tunnels have been mapped so far. The largest caves at Yucatán are called Loltun Caves, and their name derives from the Mayan words for "stone flower." Stalactites in these caves create a bell-like chime when struck, and archeological finds suggest that the caves were first inhabited 7,000 years ago.

◄ The limestone structures in the Gran Cenote are often compared to a tiny city of skyscrapers.

WONDER
No More

▼ Parts of Virunga National Park have been devastated by the clearing of land for farming using "slash-and-burn."

We are changing our planet at a rate that has only been equalled in the past by cataclysmic events, such as massive meteorite impacts and supervolcano eruptions. Only future generations will fully comprehend the damage we are doing to some of Earth's most awesome places.

War-torn wilderness

Despite suffering a century of poaching and years of war, the small population of mountain gorillas in Virunga National Park, in the Democratic Republic of the Congo, clings to life. However, the habitat is under relentless pressure from the growing human population, and large areas of forest have been destroyed.

▶ The Virunga National Park is the oldest reserve in Africa and is home to around 100 mountain gorillas.

▼ Varieties of coral create a carpet of colors. Their unusual shapes give rise to common names, such as brain, lettuce, fan, and star coral.

Watery grave

The corals of Belize have been described as the most outstanding barrier reef in the Northern Hemisphere and a significant habitat for endangered species, such as marine turtles, manatees, and American marine crocodiles.

▲ Belize corals are being bleached (killed) by a combination of pollution and rising temperatures.

Dead and gone

The Dead Sea has been shrinking for 10,000 years, but in just 25 years its area has diminished by one fifth. As more water is extracted from the River Jordan, less reaches the Dead Sea. Water is also removed for salt production.

▼ The Dead Sea is a landlocked hypersaline lake between Israel and Jordan.

▼ A pumping station removes water from the Dead Sea to evaporation pools, so salts can be extracted.

◄ Slash pines growing in the freshwater areas of Florida create a habitat for birds and small mammals. The timber is also of commercial use.

Everglades forever?

For the last 70 years, developers have been draining Florida's Everglades swamps to build on the reclaimed land, and water has been diverted from the swamps to supply agriculture and urban areas. The effects have been described as environmental ruin.

▲ Housing developments on the Everglades replace precious habitats and destroy entire ecosystems.

Amazing NATURE

Take a closer look at the must-see moments and breathtaking drama of spectacular events in the wild.

◀ Perched on the edge of a waterfall, a grizzly bear carefully balances as salmon fling themselves out of the water and into its menacing jaws.

PENGUINS
on Parade

The life of an emperor penguin demands powers of endurance far beyond our grasp. During the extremes of a polar winter, these flightless birds undertake extraordinary treks to rear their chicks and find food. They suffer starvation and endure bone-chilling blizzards in subzero temperatures.

▼ Up to 5,000 males huddle together, taking turns in the middle of the group where it is warmest.

▼ There is no nest, so the male warms the egg against a patch of bare belly skin.

Buddy body warmth
While the females feast on fish and squid, storing energy as body fat, the males huddle together for warmth and wait. Blisteringly cold winds whip around the colony. Far from the sea, the males cannot feed, and survive on stores of body fat. It will be around 64 days until the females return.

Meeting a mate
With little land in the Southern Ocean, emperor penguins must wait for sea ice to form in early winter before they can leave the water and set off on the long journey across the pack ice to the breeding colonies. Here they form pairs, and the female lays a single egg in mid-May. She transfers her egg onto its father's broad feet, and departs for the sea. He will care for the egg until she returns.

EMPEROR PENGUINS HAVE MULTIPLE LAYERS OF SCALELIKE FEATHERS THAT ARE TIGHTLY PACKED, SO ONLY THE HARSHEST WINDS CAN RUFFLE THEM.

▼ An emperor penguin can dive to depths of 1,300 ft (400 m), staying underwater for up to 20 minutes.

In their element

Upon their return to the sea, the emperors' clumsy movements on land become a distant memory. Their torpedo-shaped bodies cut through the water at up to 9 mph (around 14 km/h), and they can dive to depths where there is little or no light. No one knows how the birds find their prey in deep water that is as dark as ink.

▼ Crossing vast expanses of ice is hard work, so penguins toboggan on their bellies to save energy.

▶ Parents protect their chicks from the extreme cold and predators, such as skuas.

From fast to feast

The males must now undertake a journey of up to 60 mi (100 km) across the ice to reach open water. After feeding they return to the colony and from then on, both parent birds take turns hunting to feed their chick. When the sea ice begins to break up at the height of summer, the chicks and adults journey to the sea to forage.

Single parents

Fully fed, the females arrive back at the colony in time for the hatching of the eggs. Each male hands over his egg and heads off seaward. When the egg hatches, the chick is fed by the mother with regurgitated food.

LEAP of Faith

Ocean-swimming salmon head inland to breed and the sheer number of fish surging upriver makes for a captivating spectacle. For greedy grizzlies, however, this is a flying feast of fast-moving, protein-packed lunches—and an opportunity to enjoy some freshwater fishing.

Fast food

In summer, sockeye salmon begin the journey home—they must spawn (lay their eggs) in the rivers where they themselves hatched. Knowing a feast is on its way, grizzly bears gather by rapids and falls where the salmon leap out of the water to travel upstream, or plunge into the river to trap the fish against the river floor with their giant paws. A summer diet of salmon enables a grizzly to store enough fat to survive the winter, when it may eat very little for months.

PROTEIN PACKS

Scientists once believed there were different species of brown bear. DNA tests, however, have proved they are all the same and they share the species name of *Ursus arctos*. The variance in sizes is mostly due to the bears' diets. Kodiak bears and coastal grizzlies have access to high-protein diets.

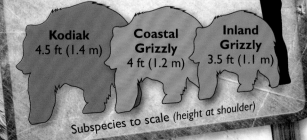

Kodiak
4.5 ft (1.4 m)

Coastal Grizzly
4 ft (1.2 m)

Inland Grizzly
3.5 ft (1.1 m)

Subspecies to scale (height at shoulder)

▶ In some places, the fish are so numerous that a bear merely has to stand with its mouth open to catch a salmon as it flings itself through the air.

Need to breed

As they travel, the salmon change from silvery blue to bright red, with greenish heads. The color develops in their skins, not their scales (which are transparent) and signifies that they are ready to mate. Ten million sockeyes may migrate up just one river in a single spawning season, turning sections of the watercourse into a cauldron of thrashing scarlet bodies. These salmon will never make the journey again—they reproduce only once in their lives.

▲ The salmon swim upstream and the females search for a suitable place to lay their eggs in the gravel, in hollows called redds.

▶ The salmon die, but their rotting bodies return nutrients to the habitat, helping to feed the fry (young fish) and other animals in the river.

Onward and upward

The salmon hordes soldier on, but their numbers fall with every grizzly onslaught. Eventually, the survivors reach the upstream gravel beds. Females release their eggs while the males fertilize them. Soon both parents will die.

Hatch and go

After several months the eggs will hatch, and the fry stay in the river until the following summer. As young adults they begin the reverse migration, heading downstream to the ocean.

▶ A newly hatched sockeye is called an alevin. It stays in its redd for a month, and survives on food in the egg's yolk.

Butterfly
CLOUDS

Many birds make incredible journeys, but how do tiny, fragile insects survive monumental migrations of 2,000 mi (around 3,000 km)? Monarch butterflies head south for winter, but their epic odyssey is just one part of a bizarre life cycle.

▶ Each monarch adult has a long, slender proboscis (sucking mouthpart), which absorbs liquid nectar from inside the flower.

Generation X

Every year, the final summer generation of North American monarch adults (imagos) is different to those that came before. Instead of a short and predictable life spent sipping nectar and reproducing, these daredevils are fated to start the long journey to Mexico. As days shorten and the cool autumn air sweeps in, these imagos feed, store their energy, and set off.

METAMORPHOSIS

Butterflies undergo metamorphosis, transforming from caterpillars into their adult form. During the summer, the caterpillars feed on milkweed, storing its toxic, milky sap in their bodies and becoming poisonous to potential predators.

1. Fat, mature caterpillars pupate. During this time of metamorphosis their bodies will develop into adults, or imagos.

2. The pupa is suspended by a silken thread. Body parts, such as the wings and abdomen, are visible on the pupa.

3. An adult emerges from the pupa. Its body is still soft and will have to harden before the imago can fly.

A multitude of monarchs

Using the Sun as a compass and Earth's magnetic field to navigate, millions of imagos instinctively fly south. Feeding en route, the monarchs actually gain weight on their journey—possibly saving energy by gliding on air currents. They cluster together at night to rest.

▼ Countless monarchs take to the skies, traveling up to 80 mi (around 130 km) per day.

Ready to roost

Reaching warmer roosting places is the aim of the entire journey as, being cold-blooded, the butterflies would struggle to survive the cold winters of northern areas. Imagos often select the same roosting trees chosen by previous generations, but no one knows how they do this. The Mexican forests prove to be the perfect environment for resting insects—cool enough for their metabolisms to slow down but not so cold as to freeze them.

◄ When butterflies roost they go into a form of suspended animation (a state of near inactivity), slowly utilizing their stores of body fat. Some may fall to the forest floor, others risk being eaten by birds.

► The monarchs' winter home was a mystery until some were tagged to monitor migrations and populations.

TAG@KU.EDU
MONARCH WATCH
1-888-TAGGING
GJE 148

Homeward bound

Spring warmth wakens the butterflies. They become more active, and start to feed and mate. They begin the journey northward, later joined by their offspring, who complete the final leg of the migration.

BEACH Party

Drawn by the light of the Moon, thousands of olive ridley turtles emerge from the sea and pour onto the shore. All turtle species come onto land to lay their eggs. But only ridley turtles lay simultaneously, in a spectacular ritual that dates back millions of years.

▼ Like all reptiles, turtles breathe air. They nest on land so that their embryos can breathe while they are developing inside the eggs.

▼ Females dig their nests at their own birthplace. They usually lay up to three clutches of eggs each year.

Arribada!

The Playa Ostional in Costa Rica hosts up to 20,000 visiting female olive ridley turtles most months. Known by the locals as the Arribada ("arrival from the sea"), this mass appearance is an example of a smart reproductive strategy that is common in the natural world. By laying their fertilized eggs simultaneously, the females are hoping there is safety in numbers—for themselves and their young.

Quick dig

Although they are swift-moving and agile in water, the female turtles are cumbersome on land. They haul their heavy bodies up the beach and dig a hole in the soft sand with their flipperlike forelimbs. It's hard work, and the turtles breathe loudly and deeply as they labor. The hind limbs scoop deeper to create an egg pit, and about 100 eggs are dropped into it. The mother covers her eggs with sand and, her job done, she heads back to the sea.

▼ Newly hatched turtles head for the sea. They will stay there for up to 15 years. Females remember the smell of their beach, and return to lay their own eggs.

Hatch and dash

Baby turtles develop inside their eggs for 45 to 60 days. The ambient temperature affects their development, with lower temperatures more likely to produce males than females. When they hatch, the turtles must make a dash for the sea, avoiding any predators that lurk nearby.

▼ Fewer than one in 100 eggs hatch and the tiny turtles, with their eyes barely open, sniff the breeze and run for the sea. The run helps develop their lungs.

▼ Up to 300 people are employed to collect and sort eggs from nests at Playa Ostional.

AT ONE POINT THERE WERE FEWER THAN SEVERAL HUNDRED KEMP'S RIDLEY TURTLES LEFT. CONSERVATION EFFORTS HAVE RESTORED THE POPULATION TO 1,000 NESTING FEMALES.

Egg harvest

Playa Ostional is the only place in the world where it is legal to harvest turtle eggs. Every year, the local community harvests about four million eggs for sale and consumption. Although the harvest is controlled and regarded as sustainable, neighboring communities appear to fare better economically by conserving their turtle nests and encouraging tourism instead.

NATURE'S Nomads

H erds of wildebeest trek through African grasslands in search of food and water. Their epic journey takes them across the Mara and Gremeti rivers, where crocodiles lie in wait. The clever crocs target weak animals at the edges of the herd, so one false step could prove fatal.

Crossing the river

The wildebeest travel in a continuous circle between the southern plains of the Serengeti and the more northerly lands of the Maasai Mara. Every year they walk for about 1,800 mi (2,900 km). These marathon migrations are punctuated by dangerous river crossings, where hordes of crocodiles gather in hungry expectation.

Safety in numbers

In an overwhelming breeding spectacle, 8,000 calves may be be born in one day of the wildebeest calving season, which typically lasts for a few weeks between January and March. Each female gives birth to a single calf, surrounded by other wildebeest for protection. The calves vastly outnumber the potential predators—a breeding strategy that gives the herd a reasonable chance of maintaining its population size.

▲ Calves are usually born at the start of the rains, when conditions are most favorable. They are able to stand within 15 minutes of birth.

Quickfire crocs

Most crocodiles hunt alone. Nile crocodiles, however, have learned where wildebeest cross the rivers and adapted their behavior to enjoy a feeding bonanza. They work as a group, lining up at crossing points and waiting for the wildebeest to make a move. The crocodiles identify vulnerable individuals, block their route to the shore, and close in for the kill.

▲ A wildebeest endeavors to escape the predator's jaws, but at up to 20 ft (6 m) in length, Nile crocodiles are forceful adversaries.

ROUND ROUTE

The wildebeest leave the north in the dry season, following the rains southward to calve. They return north via pastures in the west.

KENYA
Dry season
TANZANIA
Rainy season

Now you see me...

An estimated two million grazing animals are constantly on the move across the African grassland. Most of the migrating animals are wildebeest, but about 200,000 zebras form part of this enormous cavalcade, finding protection from lions by lurking within the wildebeest herd.

▼ Zebras can only survive by constantly moving to new grazing areas. Hiding among vast wildebeest herds provides them with cover from predators.

▲ White-bearded wildebeest are one of five subspecies of blue wildebeest. They migrate in search of food, water, and phosphorous, a mineral that the females need to produce milk.

SARDINE Run

Scores of frantically working tails whisk the water along South Africa's east coast into a seething mass. Witness the sardine run—one of nature's most incredible events. This multitude of fish is a major crowd-puller and predators flock to feast here in their thousands.

▶ Cape gannets dive for fish. If they overeat they may not be able to take flight again easily, and will themselves become tasty snacks for sharks.

Chasing currents

From May to July in most years, millions of sardines are driven by their reproductive instincts to head toward their spawning grounds. Their journey takes them northward along the eastern coast of South Africa, following cool winter water currents. Scientists have suggested that the more northerly waters provide a good environment for the sardine eggs and fry (newly hatched young) to survive—and undertaking this risky journey is a price worth paying for the better start in life it gives their young.

Feeding frenzy

Numerous predators swim alongside the school, gradually forcing the sardines close to the shore and trapping them. Marlins, tuna, seals, sharks, gannets, dolphins, and whales are just some of the hungry hunters that come to enjoy the feast.

ALBATROSSES, PENGUINS, AND ORCAS MAY TRAVEL THOUSANDS OF MILES FROM THE SOUTHERN OCEAN TO FEAST ON SARDINES.

Star attraction

The only defense the massive, shimmering schools have against the predators is to close ranks, creating "bait balls" to confuse them. A tightly packed swirling circle of silvery sardines distracts some animals, but the most tenacious predators are scarcely put off by this last-ditch attempt at survival. Tourists and fishermen are drawn to the spectacle, even wading into the water with nets to catch sardines—optimistic that the prowling sharks have their eyes firmly set on a fish dinner.

▼ Fishermen look for telltale signs of sardines, such as diving birds and pods of dolphins, and can land thousands of fish in one net.

▶ A sailfish uses its bill to jab at fish in the bait ball as it swims past before rushing back in to swallow them whole.

▲ Sharks are normally solitary animals but copper, dusky, bull, ragged-tooth, and tiger sharks all appear along the sardine run.

Follow that food

The mechanics of the sardine run largely remain a mystery. A drop in ocean temperature appears to trigger the headlong rush along the coast, which explains why the run sometimes fails to occur in exceptionally warm years. The fish follow cold currents that carry huge quantities of their food, plankton, and as they swim they congregate in enormous schools, each containing millions of fish, and stretching for many miles.

FLASH Mob!

For centuries, human ancestors believed that some animal populations spontaneously arose from dust, soil, or even rotting flesh. They had witnessed the sudden, awesome appearance of thousands of animals, with no clues as to their origin.

◀ Garter snakes swarm to generate heat and keep themselves warm. This helps them to mate more readily.

Best mates

With snow still lying on the ground, the first male red-sided garter snakes waken after a winter's hibernation. The spring warmth heralds the sudden appearance of tens of thousands more, forming seething masses that wait for the emergence of the first females. This surprising spectacle is the largest gathering of reptiles in the world. As each female wakens, she finds herself surrounded by up to 50 males in a tangled heap, ready and willing to mate.

▼ An enormous swarm of mayflies takes off from the water and frenetically turns its attention to mating.

One day

Hundreds of thousands of mayflies lurk in a pond, invisible until one special day. Surviving as nymphs hidden in the pond's sediment, the mayflies feed and grow to adulthood. A change in temperature is the most likely trigger that spurs the mayflies into action. They simultaneously change into adults with wings, and surface. In their adult form, mayflies do not even live long enough to feed—they mate and die within one to three days of emerging.

Big babies

When millions of periodical cicadas hatch at the same time, scientists call the phenomenon a "mass emergence." But to anyone nearby this astonishing event means just one thing: a relentless chorus of raucous mating calls. The bugs survive underground for 13 or 17 years (depending on the species) as nymphs, feeding on tree roots. When their internal alarm clocks go off, the adults dig their way out and prepare to mate. The males sing to attract females, but it is a short swan song: they survive in their adult form for just a few weeks.

▼ Up to 1.5 million cicadas may emerge simultaneously in just one acre (4,000 sq m) of land to molt (shed their exoskeletons), mate, and die.

Spooky silk

When tent caterpillars seemingly appear from nowhere, they do it in style. Millions emerge from their tiny eggs simultaneously, smothering trees and bushes with their squirming bodies. The caterpillars surround themselves with a protective shield of silk. After gorging on leaves, they return to their tents to digest their food, untroubled by birds and other predators that are deterred by the sticky silk.

◄ Caterpillars of the ermine spindle moth swarm over a tree, stripping it of foliage and leaving a ghostly memento of their presence.

he RIVALS

Animals are driven by the need to reproduce, and this causes the males of some species to risk life and limb in an attempt to pass on their genes. Fierce competition for mates can lead to bloody battles, and breathtaking wildlife spectacles.

Fight on!

Smart animals give fair warning before launching into a fight. In elephant seals, loud roars, head shaking, and other displays of strength and size may be enough to win dominance without taking any physical risks. But if all else fails, male seals enter the ring with gusto. They rush headlong at one another and slap their heads and necks together, head-butting and biting with ferocity. Thick layers of fat and muscle around their heads and throats provide some protection, but the violent encounters usually result in injuries, and fatalities are common.

Round

1

Hercules beetle
VS.
Hercules beetle

Weapon of choice: Giant pincer horns
Damage: Can slash opponent in two

10 STRENGTH FACTOR

Regarded, for its size, as one of the strongest animals on Earth, the tropical Hercules beetle uses its pincerlike horns to grab hold of its opponent, lift it, and go for a body slam. This American mini-monster may be only 6 in (15 cm) long but it can lift 850 times its own weight. A victor wins mating rights with any female spectator.

Giraffe V Giraffe

5 STRENGTH FACTOR

Weapon of choice: Absurdly long neck
Damage: Rarely fatal

Adult male giraffes living in small groups frequently spar with one another, especially when fertile females are around. Known as necking, they fight by walloping their necks against each other and using their heads like clubs. A well-timed swing can knock an opponent to the ground, leaving it temporarily unconscious.

◄ When male elephant seals fight, they inflate their noses and roar. Their roars are so loud they can be heard from miles away.

SPANISH IBEX

8 STRENGTH FACTOR

SPANISH IBEX

Weapon of choice: Huge horns
Damage: Serious flesh wounds may lead to death

Dueling is common in horned animals, but male Spanish ibex are gladiators without equal. Males battle for mating rights, relying on their toughened skulls and muscle-packed shoulders for defense during fights, known as "ruts." Despite this protection, horns that grow to 26 in (75 cm) in length can deliver deadly wounds.

SO MACHO

In the animal world, it is not uncommon for males to try to mate with as many females as possible. To do so they may have to fight off other males, and in these instances great strength, size, and weapons are an advantage. As a result, the males of some species grow to be enormous compared to females, and often labor under impressive horns or antlers, have immensely muscular shoulders, or possess outsize fangs and claws.

▲ A male elephant seal can weigh four or five times as much as a female.

Think
PINK

Shocking pink flamingos flock to Africa's soda lakes, strutting and gliding across the rich waters. More than one million lesser flamingos arrive to feed and dance, and create what is regarded as one of the world's most beautiful sights.

Dazzling dancers

Millions of pink flamingos arrive at a soda lake to prepare for their extraordinary courtship dances. They begin by flicking their heads and flapping their wings, but soon move into a synchronized parade. Groups of marching flamingos meld into larger congregations that move so smoothly through the water that they appear to be gliding or skating. Eventually—no one knows how—pair bonds begin to form and nesting soon follows.

Soda soup

A number of soda lakes line the Great Rift Valley in Africa. The blistering heat and a high concentration of alkaline minerals in the water have created basins of caustic soda that are hostile to most forms of life. However, tiny life forms called cyanobacteria can thrive here. The population of one type, *Spirulina*, periodically explodes and turns the water to a thick, nutritious, pea-green "soup." It is favored by flamingos, which gather in large numbers to feast on a bumper crop.

▶ Tens of thousands of flamingos can descend on Kenya's Lake Bogoria at a time.

Flame birds

Flamingos are named from the Latin word *flamma*, or flame. Their extraordinary color comes from *Spirulina*, which contain carotenoid pigments. The flamingos eat the cyanobacteria and the pigments are transferred to their feathers. To feed, flamingos use their large feet to stir the water, bringing the *Spirulina* to the surface. Then they swing their heads, upside down, from side to side. Inside their mouths are thousands of thin plates that strain the tiny organisms from the water.

▼ Even while feeding, flamingos are able to keep a watchful eye open for predators.

◀ During their courtship dances, groups of male flamingos break up, reunite, and change direction simultaneously.

DANGER AHEAD!

Africa's lesser flamingos are declining in number because their soda lake ecosystems are threatened. Commercial extraction of soda ash from the lakes damages the habitat, but growing populations of people around the lakes are also having a significant impact. More water is being drawn from the rivers that feed the lakes for agricultural use, and pollution entering the lakes is on the rise.

▲ Hyenas run alongside the lake, hoping to get lucky and grab a bird as it takes off.

SWARM!

A single swarm of 20 million bats may seem a frightening prospect, but these small flying mammals are helpful, not harmful. Mexican free-tailed bats form some of the greatest congregations of animals on Earth, and tens of millions may inhabit just one cave. These colonies need an enormous quantity of food to survive, and their diet is made up entirely of insects, many of which are agricultural pests.

NIGHT FRIGHT

THE FLAPPING HORDES LEAVE THEIR ROOST TO HUNT

Invasion of the KILLER BEES

To the untrained eye, an Africanized or "killer" bee looks just like a European honeybee. Killer bees, however, are very aggressive, and quick to swarm when food is scarce, or when they want to create new nests. Swarms can detect people 50 ft (15 m) away from their nests and don't hesitate to sting in defense. They move swiftly to attack, and will even chase people some distance. While one sting is rarely fatal, hundreds of stings can prove to be lethal.

THE ACTIONS OF A SINGLE BEE, BIRD, BAT, OR BUG MAY APPEAR INSIGNIFICANT, BUT WHEN SPECIES BAND TOGETHER THEY CAN PUNCH FAR ABOVE THEIR WEIGHT AND HAVE A DRAMATIC IMPACT. THE MOST AWESOME SWARMS NUMBER MILLIONS OF INDIVIDUALS, AND MAKE FOR A SPECTACULAR SIGHT.

A TAWNY MASS HOVERS AND SWIRLS OVER THE AFRICAN SCRUBLAND...

PHENOMENAL FLOCKS

From a distance it could be mistaken for a fast-moving dust cloud, but a closer look reveals that it is actually a congregation of the world's most abundant bird—the red-billed quelea.

Thousands of these weaver birds flock to feast on seed crops and trees, stripping them bare. There are more than 1.5 billion red-billed queleas in total, and some flocks are so huge they can take five hours to pass overhead.

A SWARM OF LOCUSTS MAY NUMBER 16,000,000,000 INDIVIDUALS!

LOCUST PLAGUE!

WHEN THE POPULATION OF LOCUSTS IN AN AREA OUTGROWS THE AVAILABLE FOOD, IT'S TIME TO SWARM. . .

- A locust eats its bodyweight in food every day.
- A swarm can devour 35,000 tons of food in 24 hours.
- In 2004, around 69 billion locusts gathered in a mega-swarm, devastating parts of northwest Africa.
- A swarm can travel 80 mi (around 130 km) or more in one day.
- One long-distance migration in 1988 saw locusts travel from West Africa to the Caribbean—that's about 3,000 mi (nearly 5,000 km) in ten days.

▶ In 2004, Senegal suffered one of the world's worst locust invasions.

Marine Marvels

Some of nature's most awesome events occur beneath the surface of the sea and at its coasts. Hidden from human eyes, convoys of lobsters march across the seabed, while blooms of golden jellyfish gently propel themselves through salty waters, and colorful squid dance for their mates.

Golden jellies

Up to ten million golden jellyfish migrate in the marine lakes at Palau, in the Pacific Ocean. The saline lakes are enclosed, but still experience tidal flows because ocean water has access to them. Every morning, the jellyfish move up to the surface of the water and swim across the lake, following the course of the Sun. Sunlight is essential for the health of the algae that live inside the jellyfish and provide them with energy.

Flash dance

The Australian giant cuttlefish grows to 5 ft (1.5 m) in length. In winter, many thousands migrate to shallow waters where the males dazzle females with spectacular displays of color. The dances begin with a show of size, as the males stretch out their "arms" to prove their superiority, and zebra patterns whizz down their flanks. Like other cuttlefish, these giants can change color in an instant, and they produce a show so impressive that divers, as well as female cuttlefish, gather to enjoy the performance.

▼ A male broadclub cuttlefish shields his mate from a potential rival during their courtship ritual.

Quick march

Late summer storms spur Caribbean spiny lobsters into action. As their coastal waters cool, and low winds make the shallow waters murky, the lobsters get ready to move. Lined up in single file, the intrepid crustaceans march to deeper areas, where warm water speeds the development of the females' eggs. They will mate here, and return to the shallows in spring.

▲ Each spiny lobster touches the tail fan of the lobster in front as it walks, forming an orderly line. It's a bizarre event, and one which few people ever witness.

▼ Golden jellyfish bask in sunlight so that the microscopic algae that live inside them have access to the light rays they need to survive.

Land ahoy!

When a killer whale approaches an ice floe or land, there is little warning other than the sudden appearance of its black dorsal fin. Also known as orcas, these super predators come in search of a meaty seal takeaway. Using enormous strength and speed, orcas fling themselves onto shore to grab their prey. When a seal is resting on ice floes, an orca can tip the frozen slab, so lunch almost rolls into its mouth!

▶ An orca, despite its huge bulk, heaves itself onto shore, surprising a sea lion that has no time to escape.

SPINY LOBSTERS MIGRATE UP TO 30 MI (ABOUT 50 KM) IN A FEW DAYS. BY WALKING IN SINGLE FILE THEY REDUCE DRAG, SO THEY CAN MARCH AT DOUBLE-QUICK TIME!

NONSTOP Godwits

Many birds undertake phenomenal journeys during their seasonal migrations, but bar-tailed godwits are the most awesome of all aviators. They embark on epic nonstop journeys that take them halfway round the world.

Globetrotters

Godwits are wading birds, with an unremarkable appearance that belies their incredible stamina. They reside in the cool tundra regions of the north, where they nest and raise their chicks in summer. The birds then move southward to feed and stock up their body fat until it constitutes more than half of their bodyweight. They can then fly nonstop southward, crossing the Equator to reach feeding grounds.

Extreme endurance

Godwits migrating south never rest, eat, or drink, even though some of them are just two months old. As winter approaches in the Southern Hemisphere, the birds prepare for the return journey. Some of them may stop off in Europe en route, to enjoy milder weather than that endured by the birds that make it back to the tundra.

▶ This muscular male godwit is leaving Norway. His ultimate destination will be Australia, New Zealand, or South Africa.

The record-setter

A female godwit known as E7 was tracked undertaking the longest, fastest nonstop migratory flight in the world. After leaving New Zealand in March 2007, E7 stopped in China to rest and feed. She then flew onward to Alaska, where she raised two chicks. On August 29, E7 left for her nonstop journey back to New Zealand, and reached her feeding grounds in just eight days.

Alaska (U.S.)

CHINA

1–15 May
4,500 mi
(7,237 km)

PACIFIC OCEAN

17–24 March
6,340 mi
(10,219 km)

29 Aug–7 Sept
7,200 mi
(11,570 km)

Start/Finish

NEW ZEALAND

RED KNOT PIT-STOP

Red knots achieve a similar long distance feat to bar-tailed godwits, migrating between the southerly parts of South America and the Canadian Arctic. Each journey covers about 10,000 mi (17,000 km). They make pitstops on the way to feed and rest, but the most spectacular of these coincides with the mass arrival of horseshoe crabs at Delaware Bay in North America. The arthropods congregate to mate, and their eggs are perfect packets of protein and energy.

▲ Hordes of hungry birds, including red knots, descend on Delaware Bay, and spend several weeks gorging on horseshoe crab eggs.

SEA SWALLOWS

Arctic terns don't care that the shortest distance between two points is a straight line. Their remarkable migration between the Poles follows a figure-of-eight pattern that adds several thousand miles to their journey. The detour makes sense, because it allows the terns to save energy by traveling on the prevailing wind. Every year, a tern may fly 43,000 mi (70,000 km).

▼ Arctic terns are sometimes known as sea swallows, because of their aerobatic skills, and stamina in the sky.

ARCTIC TERNS CAN LIVE FOR UP TO 20 YEARS. ONE BIRD MAY FLY MORE THAN 200,000 MI (322,000 KM) IN ITS LIFE—THAT'S EQUIVALENT TO FLYING FROM EARTH TO THE MOON.

BLOOMING
Brilliant

Plants operate on a different timescale to animals and most reproduce, feed, and breathe without making any obvious movements or undergoing large changes. So when awesome events happen, they are especially momentous.

▲ As a titan arum flower grows it emits a nauseating smell. Its top tip eventually reaches a height of up to 10 ft (3 m) above the ground.

Sudden stench

The flowering of the stinky titan arum is unpredictable but when it happens, the event is spectacular. The tropical plant produces a massive flowering structure (called an inflorescence) from a tuber that weighs 150 lb (70 kg) or more—it's the largest tuber in the plant kingdom.

◄ The thick, leathery Rafflesia petals unfurl overnight, into a flower that measures up to 42 in (107 cm) across.

Corpse flower

The Rafflesia is said to smell of rotting flesh, but it is better known for its looks—it grows unobtrusively before erupting into the world's largest flower. However the blooming is unpredictable, and each flower lasts only a few days. Rafflesia grows as a parasite on rain forest vines and relies on small flies to pollinate its flower.

Fig feast

When a giant fig tree produces its fruit, there are rich pickings for everyone. Since these trees only fruit once every two years, the inhabitants of its Indonesian rain forest home turn up in their droves to eat their fill, including long-tailed macaques, red leaf monkeys, orangutans, gibbons, and thousands of birds. For a short while the tree becomes the hub of a noisy feasting crowd, and after a few weeks the bonanza is over.

◄ A gray gibbon swings between the branches of a fig tree to dine on its juicy fruits.

BAMBOO SHOOTS CAN GROW MORE THAN 12 IN (AROUND 30 CM) IN A SINGLE DAY, AND MAY REACH 100 FT (ABOUT 30 M) IN A SINGLE GROWING SEASON.

Burst into bloom

Bamboo forests are formed from tall-growing grasses, and once every 30 to 40 years a unique phenomenon, not yet understood by scientists, sweeps through them. It is a process called masting, when all the bamboo plants of one species spontaneously burst into flower over a large area. All the plants then simultaneously die.

▼ Giant pandas feed on bamboo. They feast during a masting event, but then face starvation when an entire bamboo forest dies afterward.

▲ Flies are trapped, turned into a tasty soup by digestive juices, and then absorbed by the plant.

Meat eater

Hidden in the boggy undergrowth in North or South Carolina, U.S., the Venus flytrap is easy to overlook. But a keen eye and great patience can be greatly rewarding: these plants are killers. Unlike most plants they do not make their food—they eat it. Their sensitive leaves form traps, and when a fly crawls inside, they respond by snapping shut—as fast as the blink of an eye.

Catch It... Kill It

Stoop and scoop

The moment when a peregrine falcon turns a hover into a stoop (power-dive) is so sudden that catching sight of it is a rare privilege for any wildlife watcher. These raptors are the fastest animals in the world, but they owe their hunting prowess as much to the accuracy of their eyesight as to their speed. A stoop brings the predator toward its aerial target at estimated speeds of over 200 mph (about 320 km/h).

TOP SECRET

▼ With forward-facing eyes, a peregrine can focus on its prey even while in a vertical dive.

Squeeze me

Some snakes take their time over lunch, and are prepared to wait weeks between meals. When the opportunity to feed arises, however, constrictor snakes are swift to strike. Once a python or boa has gripped the prey in its jaws, it wraps its huge, muscular coils around the body and slowly squeezes. This death grip forces all the air from the prey's lungs until it suffocates.

▲ A rock python can open its jaws wide enough to engulf the body of a ground squirrel.

Going in for the kill

Solitary big cats rely on stealth, speed, and strength to kill. Yet while they are supreme predators, their prey has also evolved ways to stay alive, relying on alertness, speed, and a dogged determination to survive. As many as three out of four cheetah hunts are unsuccessful, and some tigers fail to make a kill 90 percent of the time they pursue prey.

▶ A cheetah keeps its prey in its sights as it stalks to within sprinting distance.

Pack attack

Like many hunters, wolves often hunt under the cover of dark. Their natural forest habitats provide extra cover, and help these carnivores to remain hidden from even the most alert prey. Wolves usually hunt as packs of up to eight family members, and a successful hunt requires great coordination between all individuals.

▲ The alpha (dominant) pair of wolves feed first. The other pack members are only allowed to join in when the appetites of the alpha pair are sated.

Tongue tricksters

A chameleon's lightning-quick attack is so speedy that it is almost impossible to catch with the naked eye. The reptile's super-sticky tongue catapults out of its mouth at 13.4 mph (21.6 km/h), and accelerates from 0 to 20 ft (0 to 6 m) in 20 milliseconds. Even flies, which have lightning-quick reactions, are too slow to escape.

▶ The tip of a Madagascan parson's chameleon's tongue works like a small suction cup.

ONE YEAR

IN THE WILD

Every minute of every day, extraordinary events occur in the natural world. Driven by the instinct to survive, there is always an awesome spectacle to be seen somewhere. Follow a selection of nature's highlights around the globe and be amazed from January to December.

January

Many hundreds of bald eagles gather at their winter habitat at Klamath Basin marshes in Oregon, U.S. These majestic birds spend the coldest months of the year on the frozen water, feeding on waterfowl.

May

A four-hour trek through drizzle and high vegetation in the Rwandan cloud forest may be rewarded with the sight of a family of endangered mountain gorillas. Some have become accustomed to human presence, and will continue to play and eat while spectators watch.

April

Two million migratory birds gather around Broome in Western Australia to begin their 6,000 mi (10,000 km) flight to the Northern Hemisphere, along the Australasian flyway—one of the world's greatest migratory flight paths.

August

The Danum Valley in Borneo is hard to reach, but the trip deep into a rain forest is worthwhile. Watch orangutans in the wild while you can—they face extinction within 20 years because their habitat is being replaced by palm oil plantations.

September

Wish You Were Here!

Male elks in Yellowstone National Park, Wyoming, U.S., begin the rutting season. Furious fighting precedes mating.

October

February

Whale sightings are at their best in the Southern Hemisphere's summer. Minke, humpback (left), beaked, fin, southern right, and blue whales can be spotted around the Antarctic Peninsula and into the Southern Ocean. They come to feast, making the most of a temporary abundance of food.

March

Tigers are one of the world's most elusive big cats, and this is a good time to see them in the Sunderban and Ranthambore Tiger Reserves in India.

June

Sloth bears in Sri Lanka are normally nocturnal, but in June they become active in the day as well, so they can feast on the trees' ripening fruit.

July

The glorious purple emperor butterfly is an elusive woodland inhabitant. This is the best time to see it flying around the U.K.'s native oak trees.

Only the males have the resplendent purple sheen, which is created when light is refracted by the wing scales. Females are brown.

November

On clear mornings by the upper Tambopata River in Peru, hundreds of macaws arrive to lick clay from the bank. Eating earth is called "geophagy," and it occurs in several animal species. The clay contains minerals that may be useful supplements to an animal's diet.

Thousands of polar bears gather at Churchill, Manitoba in Canada. They are waiting for the Hudson River to freeze over so they can hunt.

December

In Japan, China, and Russia, Japanese red-crowned cranes gather to begin their beautiful, synchronized courtship dances.

On the HOOF

Pronghorns and caribou undertake the longest migrations of any land animals in the New World. Long ago, there may have been millions of these deer trekking across the North American plains, but interference from humans has added many obstacles to their journeys.

Going the distance

Caribou herds may number thousands, and make 3,000-mi (about 5,000-km) journeys through the course of a single year as they move to find better grazing areas, to calve, and to avoid the winter's worst weather and the summer's biting insects. Caribou can be flexible in their routes, so one year's migration might differ in route and distance from the previous year's, and may involve crossing water as well as land. Caribou can swim very well, and their winter coats have hollow hairs, which help the deer to float high in the water.

Following the food

Further north, vast herds of caribou conduct their migrations with much less interference from people. Also known as reindeer, these hoofed mammals trek through the Arctic tundra and boreal regions, where food and humans are scarce, although caribou territories once extended much further south.

▶ Caribou from the Porcupine Herd forge onward in Alaska. Their progress is tracked by satellite so that scientists can document their migratory patterns.

▼ Bison are now being allowed to exercise their migration instincts. Until recently they were confined to national parks, such as Yellowstone in Wyoming, U.S.

Buffalo woes

Yellowstone National Park, in Wyoming, U.S., is home to one of the largest free-roaming herds of bison (also known as "buffalo"). They are direct descendants of the 30 million bison that once populated the Great Plains, before relentless hunting saw their numbers fall to just 1,091 in 1889. Efforts to conserve bison often fail when the animals' instinct to migrate puts them into conflict with farmers.

◄ Many caribou migration routes require the herds to cross sizeable rivers.

Obstacle course

There are about half a million pronghorns in Wyoming, U.S.—about the same as the number of people. But almost 80 percent of the animals' ancient routes between winter feeding and summer calving grounds have disappeared beneath commercial developments. Now only one herd makes the seasonal journey, and the 100-mi (160-km) route tests the pronghorns' endurance to the limit. The natural landscape has been broken up by urbanization and roads to such an extent that reaching the calving ground is now an unnaturally hazardous exercise.

▼ Pronghorns cross busy roads and squeeze through barbed wire fences to reach their summer home.

ELEPHANTS
on the March

Elephants walk with intent when they are on the move. Driven by the need for water and food, a herd on the march creates a majestic procession that seems to operate with a single mind. These extremely intelligent animals are highly social and have strong family bonds.

ELEPHANTS CAN COMMUNICATE WITH EACH OTHER BY MAKING LOW-FREQUENCY RUMBLES. THE SOUNDS PASS THROUGH THE GROUND TO HERD MEMBERS, WHICH HEAR THE RUMBLES THROUGH THEIR FEET.

▼ As the length and severity of droughts in parts of Africa increase, herds of desert elephants spend their days wandering in search of water.

BIG APPETITES

An adult elephant needs to eat 350 lb (160 kg) of food every day, and may tear down branches to get fruit, strip bark, and even fell whole trees to feed. When a herd of these huge animals is confined to a small area it can inadvertently demolish its own food source, which is why elephants need massive territories, and many of them migrate to survive.

DROUGHT AND DEATH

The search for water is a powerful motivator in arid regions of Africa. During the dry seasons, river courses become dusty tracks of rubble and sand for months on end, so elephants must endure blistering heat, dust storms, and near starvation to reach the ever-dwindling waterholes.

▶ Elephants use their trunks to reach deep into waterholes in search of water. They may also find sodium in the water and surrounding rock. This essential mineral is lacking in the diet of many elephants in arid areas, so they eat soil or lick rock to get it.

▼ Elephants follow safe routes between waterholes and neighboring national parks and tourists congregate to view the spectacle.

ON THE RIGHT ROAD

The future is looking good for Namibia's migrating elephants—the largest elephant population in Africa. Since the value of the herds to the ecosystem and tourism has been appraised, conservation has been put high on the national agenda. Corridors—the pathways followed by migrating elephants—are now protected. Elephants in different areas face different problems, so conservation efforts have to be tailor-made to fit each region.

TEMPERATURES SOAR TO 120°F (49°C) IN MALI'S SAHEL REGION, WHILE ELEPHANTS COMPLETE ROUND TRIPS OF 300 MI (480 KM) EVERY YEAR TO FIND WATER AND FOOD.

▼ Up to ten African elephants descend on this Zambian lodge every October when the mango trees fruit. The hotel now encourages guests to enjoy the spectacle.

ELEPHANT IN THE ROOM

When hotels are built on ancient elephant corridors, the animals do not always understand that they should take a detour. A herd of elephants was not deterred by the erection of Mfuwe Lodge at South Luangwa National Park in Zambia— they simply walked right through the hotel's reception to reach the fruiting mango trees they have been visiting for generations.

Body SCIENCE

Take a top-to-toe tour of the human anatomy, from amazing microscopic views to X-rays of the body in action.

◄ A scanning electron microscope (SEM) reveals a clot of red and white blood cells in a blood vessel.

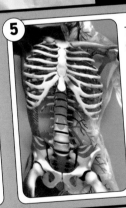

Building
THE BODY

The body is made up of 12 different, interlinking systems—each one performs a particular task, but they are all dependent on each other. Some, such as the circulatory system, spread throughout the body. Others, such as the digestive system, are mainly in one place.

1
The **digestive system** breaks down food into chemicals that the body can absorb and use for fuel and materials, and then removes the rest as waste. It includes the stomach, intestines, and anus.

2
The **urinary system** removes excess water as urine. It also gets rid of impurities in the blood. It includes the kidneys and bladder.

INNARDS

3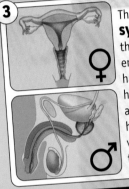
The **reproductive system** consists of the sex organs that enable humans to have children. Males have a penis, scrotum, and testicles. Females have a uterus, cervix, vagina, fallopian tubes, and ovaries.

FRAMEWORK AND WEATHERPROOFING

4
The **muscular system** is made up of three types of muscle—skeletal, smooth, and heart. It circulates blood around the body and enables it to move.

5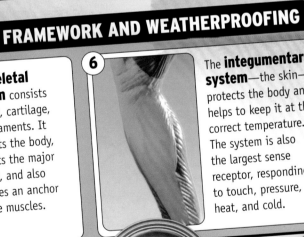
The **skeletal system** consists of bone, cartilage, and ligaments. It supports the body, protects the major organs, and also provides an anchor for the muscles.

6
The **integumentary system**—the skin—protects the body and helps to keep it at the correct temperature. The system is also the largest sense receptor, responding to touch, pressure, heat, and cold.

WIRING AND CONTROL

7
The **nervous system** contains the brain and the nerves. The brain receives electrical signals from the body via nerves and quickly sends back a response.

8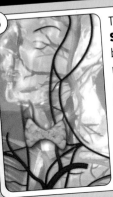
The **endocrine system** controls body processes. It releases floods of chemical messages called hormones into the blood from glands around the body.

PIPING

9 The **respiratory system**—the airways and lungs—takes air into the lungs to supply oxygen to the body. It also breathes out the waste gas, carbon dioxide.

10 The **circulatory system** includes the heart and the network of blood vessels. It carries blood from the heart to all the body cells, and back again. Blood circulates continuously around the body.

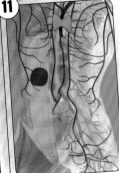
11 The **lymphatic system** is the body's "sewage" works, draining excess fluid and debris from the immune system. It contains a network of tubes that run throughout the body.

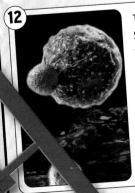
12 The **immune system** defends the body against invading germs and repairs damage. It includes barriers, such as the skin, white blood cells, and antibodies.

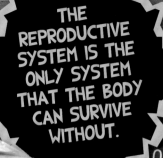
THE REPRODUCTIVE SYSTEM IS THE ONLY SYSTEM THAT THE BODY CAN SURVIVE WITHOUT.

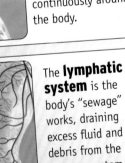

Body s

WILD Landscape

Powerful microscopes have revealed the surface of the body to be surprisingly varied. Close-up, skin looks like rough terrain and hair grows on it like a forest. The skin is such an important organ that it receives more than one third of the body's blood supply.

Hair-raising

Humans are one of the few land mammals to have almost bare skin, so we wear clothes to keep warm. This bare skin, however, helps to keep the body cool. The 100,000 hairs on our heads grow faster than anything else on the body—and under a microscope they look like bumpy tree trunks.

▼ Although just 2 mm thick, the skin is made of various layers.

Scalp hairs grow 2–3 mm each week. Each hair grows for three to five years before it falls out, and a new hair starts to grow.

Mighty overcoat

The skin is the biggest organ in the body and has many important functions. It's waterproof and germproof, insulates the body from the cold and lets out excess heat, responds to touch, and gives the body nourishment by soaking up vitamin D from sunlight.

Shedding skin

To stay effective, skin has to be continually renewed. New cells push up from the dermis to provide the outer layer of protective dead cells in the epidermis. The body loses 40,000 of these dead cells every minute. In a human's lifetime, nearly 100 lb (50 kg) of skin is lost.

ROLLED OUT FLAT, YOUR SKIN WOULD COVER 21 SQ FT (2 SQ M). IT WEIGHS 9 LB (4 KG).

Nailing it

Just like hair, nails are made from a tough material called keratin, created when certain cells die and harden. Fingernails grow about 1.5 in (3.5 cm) a year—so, uncut, they could grow 10 ft (3 m) or more in a lifetime. The middle fingernail grows fastest and the thumbnail grows slowest.

▶ The nail plate—the visible part of the nail—is made of a hard, transparent type of keratin.

The outer layer of the skin, or **epidermis**, is a tough coating of overlapping layers of dead skin cells.

Underneath, in the **dermis**, there's a thicker layer containing glands, nerve endings, and touch sensors.

Under that, there's a blanket of fat, called "**subcutaneous fat**," to keep the body warm.

The dermis and fat layers are well supplied with **blood**.

▶ As old skin cells die, they leave a hard protein called keratin on the outside of the skin. Keratin gives the skin a tough, protective outer coat, which eventually flakes off.

GROWING SKIN

Artificial skin can be grown in laboratories. It is used to treat people who have suffered severe burns or skin diseases, as well as for testing the effects of drugs and cosmetics.

▶ Each piece of artificial skin is usually grown from a tiny piece of human skin.

CELLuLaR Cosmos

The body is made up of 100 trillion microscopic parcels called cells. They come in many shapes and sizes as soft cases of chemicals, each with its own personal set of life instructions in the form of DNA.

SCIENTISTS ESTIMATE THAT ONLY FIVE PERCENT OF THE BODY'S CELLS BELONG TO THE BODY—THE REST ARE BACTERIA.

SOME TYPES OF CELL AUTOMATICALLY DIE WHEN THEY BECOME DAMAGED.

THE CELL ZOO

There are more than 200 different kinds of body cell, such as fat cells and skin cells, each with its own special task. The smallest cells are granules in the brain, and the longest are nerve cells that run through the spinal cord from the brain to the toes.

BLOOD CELLS carry oxygen around the body.

MUSCLE CELLS contract to enable the body to move.

NERVE CELLS carry messages between the brain and the body.

BONE CELLS make bone harden as it forms.

SPERM CELLS carry the male's genes to the egg.

OVUM CELLS contain the female genes, ready for fertilization.

THE SMALLEST CELLS ARE RED BLOOD CELLS AT ONLY 0.0075 MM ACROSS.

Working hard

Every cell is a bustling chemical factory, working every second of the day. Inside each cell, a team of "organelles" perform different tasks. Some transport chemicals to and fro, some break up chemicals, and some make new chemicals, use them, and send them off to other cells. The overall instructions come from the nucleus, but every organelle knows its task.

◄ The inside of a cell, magnified millions of times, shows some of its different features.

THE LARGEST CELLS ARE NERVE CELLS AND CAN REACH 3 FT (ONE METER) IN LENGTH.

SOME CELLS IN THE GUTS LIVE FOR ONLY A FEW DAYS, WHILE PANCREATIC CELLS CAN LIVE FOR AS LONG AS ONE YEAR.

Anatomy of a cell

1 **Ribosomes** (red dots) continually make amino acids to build new proteins.

2 **Rough endoplasmic reticulum** is a series of sheets in which ribosomes operate.

3 **Cytoskeleton** is the framework of protein threads within the cell wall that hold the cell together.

4 **Nucleus** determines what proteins will be made. It includes the basic program of DNA, twisted into bundles called chromosomes.

5 **Mitochondria** transform chemical compounds into the cell's fuel, called ATP.

6 **Vacuoles** carry newly assembled proteins from the rough endoplasmic reticulum to the Golgi apparatus for dispatch.

7 **Lysosomes** are responsible for breaking down and dealing with materials taken in by the cell.

8 **Cytoplasm** is the liquid-filled space inside the cell, in which the organelles float.

9 **Golgi apparatus** prepares new proteins for use around the body.

CHEMICAL Plant

The body is made from a mixture of water and organic chemicals, and contains more than half the known chemical elements in the Universe. Every part of the body is involved in changing one chemical to another.

You're wet

The body is more than 60 percent water, found both in cells and body fluids such as blood and lymph. Without water for chemicals to dissolve in, vital reactions could not take place.

You're fat

Much of the body is simply fat. "Essential fat" is needed for particular body tasks—making up 3–5 percent of men's bodies and 8–12 percent of women's. "Storage fat" is fat built up as adipose tissue to give the body an energy reserve. Pads of fat also help to keep out the cold and act as shock absorbers.

▲ Adipose cells are packed with lipids (fat), which store emergency energy reserves.

You're strong

Chemicals called proteins make up about 20 percent of the body. Some proteins are building materials—every cell and tissue is part-protein, including muscles, bones, tendons, hair, nails, and skin. Other proteins make chemical reactions happen (enzymes), send chemical messages (hormones), fight infection (antibodies), or carry oxygen in the blood (hemoglobin).

▶ Blue and red fluorescent dyes show up the protein in throat tissue.

You're sweet

Carbohydrates provide fuel, either circulating in the blood ready for action as simple sugars, or stored as glycogen in the liver and the muscles.

◄ The uterine gland in a pregnant woman's womb secretes glycogen to give the egg energy to grow.

You're made to plan

Nucleic acids are the body's programmers. Deoxyribonucleic acid (DNA) in every cell, passed on from your parents, stores the instructions that tell the body not only how to grow, but also what to do throughout life.

► A sample of DNA that has been extracted from body cells.

You're a mineral mine

Bones are partly made of the minerals calcium and phosphorus. Calcium and sodium in the blood, and phosphorus, potassium, and magnesium in the cells, are essential for chemical processes. Iron is crucial to hemoglobin, which carries oxygen in the blood. Traces of other minerals are also vital, including cobalt, copper, iodine, manganese, and zinc.

► The calcium in cheese (magnified here) strengthens bones.

You're a gas

The body contains gases, such as oxygen, carbon dioxide, nitrogen oxide, hydrogen, carbon monoxide, and methanethiol. Some are dissolved in fluids and others are bubbles of gas in the lungs or gut.

BODY CHEMICALS

About 99 percent of the mass of the human body is made up of just six elements:

CHEMICAL	%	FOUND
Oxygen	65%	Liquids and tissues, bones, proteins
Carbon	18%	Everywhere
Hydrogen	10%	Liquids and tissues, bones, proteins
Nitrogen	3%	Liquids and tissues, bones, proteins
Calcium	1.5%	Bones, lungs, kidney, liver, thyroid, brain, muscles, heart
Phosphorus	1%	Bones, urine

VITAL

Blood is the body's circulation and transport system. It not only delivers oxygen from the lungs to every body cell, it also carries food to fuel and maintain cells, collects and washes away waste, keeps up to the level of hormones and things the body needs. Blood rushes fighting cells into action to defend against infection, and even helps to spread the body heat...

▼ Scabs are the body's way of protecting a wound from infection.

Plugging a leak

When you cut yourself and bleed from the damaged blood vessels, platelets instantly gather. As they do, they send out an alarm in the form of "clotting factors." These draw in other platelets and encourage them to clump together to make fibers or "fibrin" that plug the leak. The fibrin dries out to form a scab, protecting the wound until it has healed.

▲ Blood cells and fibrin (yellow) rush to a wound to form a clot. This is called coagulation.

Fresh Frozen Plasma (CPD-A1)

129169J 6

O RhPOSITIVE

COMPLEX MIXTURE

Blood looks red in color, but it is mostly made up of a clear, yellowish fluid called plasma. The color red comes from the red blood cells that are swept along by it. Plasma also contains giant white cells called leucocytes and little lumps called platelets.

▼ Blood vessels have muscular walls that control the flow of blood around the body.

Super pipes

Blood circulates through millions of blood vessels—tiny pipes that thread through the body. From the heart, they branch out from wide arteries into narrow arterioles, and then even narrower capillaries. On the way back to the heart, blood vessels gather in narrow venules and then wider veins.

A mighty pump

The heart is a tireless pump, made almost entirely of muscle. Its muscular walls contract and relax about 70 times a minute, pushing all the blood around the body once every 90 seconds. The heart has two sides—the right side is smaller and weaker, and pumps blood only to the lungs. The stronger left side pumps blood around the whole body.

Seeing red

Button-shaped red blood cells contain a special chemical called hemoglobin, which carries oxygen around the body. The average person has 25 trillion red cells, and the body makes two million new ones every second.

◀ An arteriogram is an X-ray where a special dye is used to detect the heart's blood vessels.

Body SCIENCE

87

Body Heat

The body cannot survive for long without the continuous input of energy from food. Energy drives all the body's chemical reactions, which release heat energy for warmth and muscle energy for movement.

▼ Some cells only contain one mitochondrion, but others contain thousands.

◄ A thermogram detects heat. Red shows the hottest parts and blue the coldest. The head and chest are the warmest parts of the body.

A trillion fires

Tiny bursts of energy are constantly released inside each of the trillions of body cells in a process called cellular respiration. In each cell, microscopic "furnaces" called mitochondria use oxygen to break down glucose molecules and release energy. This process generates heat.

STORED ENERGY IS PACKED INTO MILLIONS OF TINY MOLECULES CALLED ATP (ADENOSINE TRIPHOSPHATE). ATP IS LIKE A COILED SPRING, READY TO UNWIND AND RELEASE ITS ENERGY.

Hot bodies

For body processes to function well, the body must remain at the perfect temperature—98.6°F (37°C). This is warmer than the outside world, so the body continually generates heat by moving the muscles and triggering chemical reactions in the liver.

ENERGY FOOD

Energy comes from carbohydrates in food, including sugar and starch. Fats in food provide energy, too, but this is stored rather than used immediately. Energy-rich molecules are either delivered to every body cell as glucose in the blood, or temporarily held in the liver as glycogen.

▼ When people play sports, the body sweats to release heat energy.

Stay cool

If the body becomes too hot, the hypothalamus (the brain's "thermostat") tells the body to lose heat by sweating through the skin's pores. Sweating not only takes warm water out of the body, but also cools the skin as the moisture evaporates. The hypothalamus also boosts the supply of blood to the skin to take heat away from the body's core.

Brrrrrrrr...

If the body becomes too cold, the hypothalamus generates heat by boosting cell activity and making the muscles move rapidly in shivers. It also cuts heat loss by restricting the supply of blood to the skin to keep warmth in the body's core.

DURING A MATCH, A TOP TENNIS PLAYER USES ENOUGH ENERGY TO BOIL A KETTLE EVERY MINUTE.

▲ In 2005, Lewis Gordon Pugh broke the world record for the farthest-north, long-distance swim, by swimming one kilometer through water in cracks between the North Pole ice.

ROUGH SKIN

When the body is cold, hairs on the skin may stand on end, creating "goose bumps." This traps a layer of warm air next to the skin, making the body feel warmer.

Human COMPUTER

The brain contains more than 100 billion nerve cells, or neurons. Each neuron is connected to as many as 25,000 other neurons—creating trillions of routes for signals to buzz around the body. This enables us to think and learn, jump and sit, and laugh and cry—everything that makes us human.

RECEIVING SIGNALS

The cerebral cortex is the wrinkled layer of interconnected nerve cells around the outside of the brain. It is made up of different structures, each with individual functions. Many sense signals are received and responded to here.

The demanding brain

The brain makes up less than two percent of the body's weight, yet demands more than 20 percent of its blood supply. Deprived of the oxygen blood carries for even a few moments, brain cells quickly die. If the blood supply is cut off entirely, the brain loses consciousness in ten seconds and death occurs within a few minutes.

Blood floods into the brain continuously through large arteries to give it energy for thinking.

PREFRONTAL CORTEX
is involved with memory, solving problems, and judgment.

A brain of two halves

The brain is split into two halves or hemispheres, linked by a bundle of nerves. The left half controls the right side of the body and the right half controls the left side of the body. It is believed that the left side deals with logical and analytical thinking, while the right side expresses emotion and creativity.

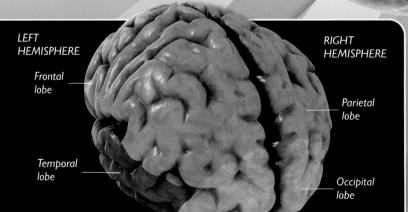

LEFT HEMISPHERE

RIGHT HEMISPHERE

Frontal lobe

Parietal lobe

Temporal lobe

Occipital lobe

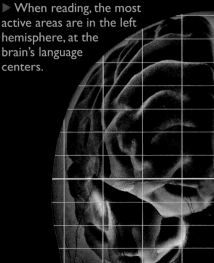

► When reading, the most active areas are in the left hemisphere, at the brain's language centers.

The gray matter

The cerebral cortex is sometimes called the "gray matter." It's where most conscious thoughts occur and its folds allow a number of nerves to be packed into a small space. Scans have revealed that it contains "association areas"— areas that become more active while we're doing certain tasks.

LIMBIC SYSTEM processes smells, emotions, and memories, which is why smells can evoke memories.

MOTOR CORTEX controls the movement of muscles around the body.

SENSORY CORTEX registers sense signals from around the body such as pressure, heat, and pain.

WERNICKE'S AREA controls the understanding of both spoken and written words.

VISUAL CORTEX analyzes what the eyes see.

HIPPOCAMPUS is involved with moods, willpower, recognizing new experiences, and short-term memory.

ON AVERAGE, A FEMALE'S BRAIN WEIGHS 2.5 PERCENT OF HER BODY WEIGHT, AND A MALE'S 2 PERCENT.

HYPOTHALAMUS controls body temperature, water levels, and blood flow. It also triggers feelings such as hunger and anger.

CEREBELLUM is the plum-sized extension of the brain that controls the body's balance and posture, and coordinates movement.

Body
SIGNALING

Nerves make up the body's communication network. They carry instant messages from the brain to every part of the body—and stream back a constant flow of data to tell the brain what's going on both inside the body and in the outside world.

Body network

The central nervous system is made up of the brain and the spinal cord—the nerves in the spine. It is responsible for collecting information fed in through nerves from all over the body, processing data, and sending out responses. The nerves of the peripheral nervous system branch out from the central nervous system to every limb and body part.

Bundle of nerves

The brain stem, spinal cord, and branches of the peripheral nervous system are made of long bundles of nerve fibers called nerves. These bundles are made from the axons (tails) of nerve cells, bound together like the wires in a telephone cable. Signals can travel at up to 395 ft (120 m) per second.

▲ Nerve fibers are bundled together and insulated by a sheath of fatty myelin to keep the signal strong.

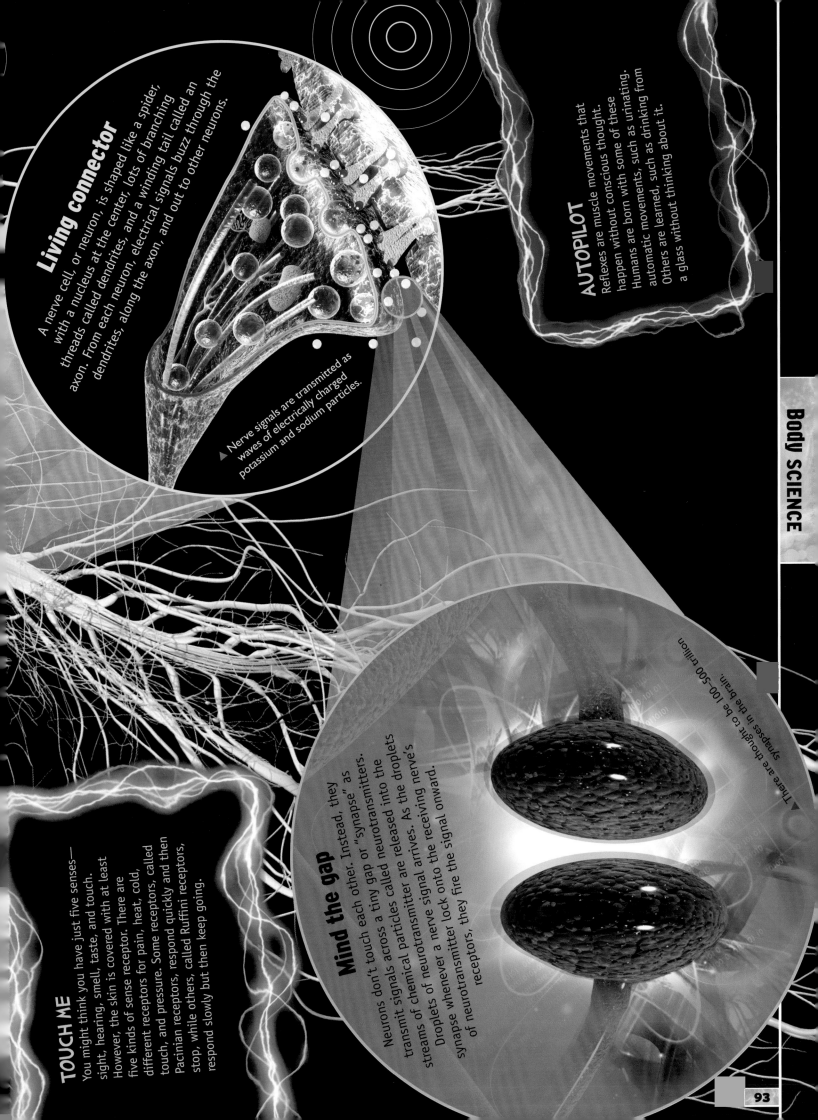

Living connector

A nerve cell, or neuron, is shaped like a spider, with a nucleus at the center. lots of branching threads called dendrites, and a winding tail called an axon. From each neuron, electrical signals buzz through the dendrites, along the axon, and out to other neurons.

▶ Nerve signals are transmitted as waves of electrically charged potassium and sodium particles.

AUTOPILOT

Reflexes are muscle movements that happen without conscious thought. Humans are born with some of these automatic movements, such as urinating. Others are learned, such as drinking from a glass without thinking about it.

TOUCH ME

You might think you have just five senses—sight, hearing, smell, taste, and touch. However, the skin is covered with at least five kinds of sense receptor. There are different receptors for pain, heat, cold, touch, and pressure. Some receptors, called Pacinian receptors, respond quickly and then stop, while others, called Ruffini receptors, respond slowly but then keep going.

Mind the gap

Neurons don't touch each other. Instead, they transmit signals across a tiny gap or "synapse." As streams of chemical particles called neurotransmitters transmit signals across a tiny gap or "synapse." As the droplets of neurotransmitter arrives. As the receiving nerve's synapse whenever a nerve signal arrives. As the receiving nerve's receptors, they fire the signal onward.

Droplets of neurotransmitter lock onto the receiving signal

▶ There are thought to be 100–500 trillion synapses in the brain.

EYE OPENER

YOUR AWESOME EYES COMBINE THE PICTURE QUALITY OF THE BEST DIGITAL CAMERAS WITH A VERSATILITY THAT NO CAMERA CAN MATCH. THEY CAN FOCUS BOTH ON A SPECK OF DUST INCHES AWAY AND A GALAXY FAR ACROSS THE UNIVERSE, AND WORK IN BOTH STARLIGHT AND SUNLIGHT.

20/70

20/50

Black hole

The dark "pupil" is a porthole that lets light into the eye. It looks black because the eye is so dark inside. When light gets very dim, the fringe or "iris" around it can open wide to let more light in.

▼ The pattern of fibers in the iris is unique to each human, so it can be used to identify individuals, just like fingerprints.

▼ A damaged cornea can cause blurred vision. To restore normal eyesight, surgeons lift the top layer of the cornea and trim it minutely with a laser.

Stay sharp

The cornea is the transparent window at the front of the eye that gives the main focusing power. Light rays pass through the cornea and are refracted (bent) before hitting the lens. The lens adjusts the focus to give a sharp picture, whether you are looking at something close-up or far away. Each adjustment takes barely one fiftieth of a second.

Movie time

The inside of the eyeball is like a mini cinema. The cornea and lens project an image onto the back of the eye, called the retina. Although the image is just a few millimeters across inside the eye, you see it at its real size.

▲ When the muscles surrounding the lens contract, the lens becomes thicker and can focus on close-up objects.

▶ There are only seven colors in the rainbow, but the eye's cones can distinguish ten million colors!

Taking the picture

The retina acts like the photocells in a camera—150 million rods detect if it's dark or light, and even work in very low light, while eight million cones detect colors and work best in daylight.

Highway to the brain

It's actually the brain that "sees," not the eyes, using the visual cortex. When light hits the retina, the rods and cones send nerve signals down the optic nerve to create a picture in the brain.

▶ Signals from the right side of each retina go to the right of the visual cortex; those from the left of each retina go to the left of the visual cortex.

NEW Life

The human body can create a new version of itself. It starts when two single, microscopically tiny cells—a male's sperm cell and a female's egg cell—join. From this combined cell a new life begins, as a baby slowly grows inside the female's womb for the nine months of pregnancy.

Sperm cells swim toward the egg cell and try to penetrate it to release the genetic material contained in their heads.

AFTER ONLY ONE WEEK, THE EMBRYO CONTAINS HUNDREDS OF CELLS.

Fertilized egg to embryo

As soon as the sperm and egg join successfully, the egg is fertilized, and the new life is "conceived." The egg immediately begins to divide rapidly, making seemingly identical copies of itself to create an embryo. As the cells multiply, differences appear, and layers that will become skin and organs develop.

Day 1

Millions try, but in most cases, only one sperm cell will succeed and fertilize the egg cell.

Day 6

The ball of cells attaches to the lining of the female's womb.

Day 40

In the beginning

The sperm and egg are special not because they have something extra, but because they have something missing. Unlike other body cells, they have only one set of 23 chromosomes, not the usual two. The sperm must add its 23 chromosomes to the egg's 23 chromosomes to make the full complement of 46 and start a new life. This happens during sexual intercourse, when the male's sperm swim into the female's womb to reach the egg.

IF TWO EGGS ARE RELEASED AT THE SAME TIME AND ARE BOTH FERTILIZED, NON-IDENTICAL TWINS DEVELOP.

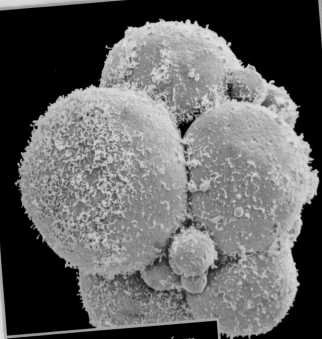

The fertilized egg divides to form a small bundle of cells.

Embryo to fetus

After about 40 days, the embryo, though barely as big as a pea, has developed some recognizable features, such as a nose, mouth, and ears. Dark spots show where the eyes will grow. A heart beats rapidly inside, and a brain, muscles, and bones start to grow. After nine weeks, the embryo has become so babylike (though with a giant head) that it is described as a fetus, not an embryo.

At this early stage, the embryo looks like a tadpole.

The fetus turns upside-down with its head toward the entrance of the womb, ready to be born.

Growing strong

At the halfway stage, the fetus looks like a curled-up baby, only smaller and less defined. It's only about the size of an adult's hand, so still has some way to grow, but it begins to move around and may even kick its developing legs inside the mother's womb. Research suggests the baby may even be able to hear things outside its mother's body.

Time for birth

Finally, after about 37 weeks, the fetus is fully developed. Birth begins when the mother goes into "labor." Firstly, the womb muscles contract and burst the bag of fluid that surrounds the baby. Secondly, the muscles around the womb's neck contract and relax rhythmically to push the baby out through the birth canal.

The embryo is now about 5 mm long and buds for the arms and legs start to develop.

Day 133
The fetus is now about 6.5 in (16 cm) long and fine, downy hair covers its body.

Day 266
The fetus is about 14 in (36 cm) long and has a firm grip.

An ultrasound scanner reveals the baby growing inside the womb.

THE YOUNGEST BABY TO BE BORN AND SURVIVE WAS ONLY 21 WEEKS OLD.

GROWTH Factor

The rate at which the body grows depends on age and gender—babies and teenagers grow rapidly, and males become taller than females. Body proportions also develop with age—a baby's legs only make up one quarter of its length, but by adulthood the legs equal half of the body's height.

Big head

A newborn baby's head is already three-quarters of its adult size because it contains the brain. There are two gaps called fontanelles between the bones of a baby's skull, where there is only membrane (a "skin" of thin tissue), not bone. This allows the skull to flex, so there is room for the brain to grow even more. The gaps close and the bones join together after about 18 months.

BABIES HAVE A MUCH STRONGER SENSE OF SMELL THAN ADULTS.

Time to grow

Children grow quickly because the brain is continually sending out a "grow-faster" chemical. This growth hormone is secreted by the pituitary gland in the center of the brain. It tells cells to make protein and break down fat for energy. Too much growth hormone can cause a condition called gigantism, or acromegaly where the body grows too big and in the wrong places.

6 months–1 year

A baby begins to grow teeth—the upper and lower incisors come first.

1–4 years

Toddlers start to talk from one year old and can read simple words from four years old.

9–13 years

◀ For the first nine months or more, babies can only move on their hands and knees.

◀ Toddlers only gradually develop the strength and balance to walk upright.

Big changes

Puberty is the time of life when humans mature sexually. This process begins at about ten years old for girls and 13 for boys. During puberty, girls grow breasts and pubic hair. The hips grow wider and a new egg is released every month, in a cycle called menstruation. Boys grow pubic and facial hair, and the testes grow and start to produce sperm. By the time a boy is 15 or so, the testes make 200 million sperm a day.

◀▼ As boys grow, they develop more muscle than girls.

▶ Humans become shorter as they get older because the vertebrae in their backs become more compressed.

FRENCHWOMAN JEANNE CALMENT (1875–1997) LIVED FOR 122 YEARS AND 164 DAYS.

◀ Adult men are on average 6 in (15 cm) taller than women.

During adolescence a boy grows about 3.75 in (9.5 cm) a year and a girl 3.35 in (8.5 cm).

20+ years

Early adulthood is from 20 to 39 years and "middle age" is from 40 to 59 years.

60+ years

In old age, eyesight and hearing often weaken.

All grownup

By the age of 20, the body is fully developed and at its physical peak. By the early 30s, the body begins to lose strength, speed, and agility. Between the ages of 45–55, most women go through the menopause and become unable to get pregnant naturally.

Old age

As the body grows older, it stops renewing itself so well—the muscles weaken, bones become more brittle, joints stiffen, and the skin starts to slacken and wrinkle. The hair may eventually turn gray as pigment cells stop working.

MUSCLE
Power

Every move the body makes needs muscles, from lifting a finger to jumping in the air—even for sitting still. Without muscles, the body would slump like a sack of potatoes. Muscles are amazing little motors that work instantly, whenever they are needed, by constantly contracting and relaxing.

IF ALL THE MUSCLES IN THE BODY PULLED TOGETHER, THEY COULD LIFT A BUS.

Running on air

Ideally, muscles work aerobically—the cells get enough oxygen from glucose to release energy. However, if a person is unfit or has worked the muscles too hard, the cells may burn glucose "anaerobically"—without oxygen. This uses up glucose rapidly, making the body tired and leaving a buildup of lactic acid, which makes the muscles sore. To draw in the extra oxygen needed to burn this lactic acid, you pant when you stop running.

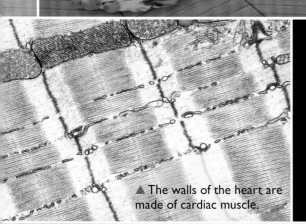

▲ The walls of the heart are made of cardiac muscle.

Outside and in

The body has two kinds of muscle—voluntary muscles that are under conscious control and involuntary muscles that work automatically. Voluntary muscles cover the skeleton and allow the body to move. Involuntary muscles control bodily functions, such as the heartbeat.

Power stripes

Muscles get their power from bundles of fibers that contract and relax. Inside each fiber are alternating, interlocking stripes or "filaments" of actin and myosin. When the brain tells a muscle to contract, little buds on each myosin filament twist, pulling on the actin filaments and making the muscle shorter. Each time a muscle contracts, another muscle fiber needs to shorten in the opposite direction to pull it back to its original length.

▶ Muscles work in pairs of actin and myosin filaments because they can only shorten themselves.

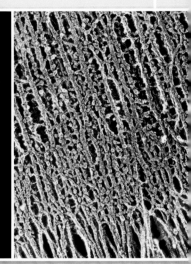

THE STRONGEST MUSCLES ARE THE MASSETER MUSCLES, WHICH CONTROL THE JAW'S BITING MOVEMENT.

▲ The body has several layers of muscle. Most are attached to bones with tough fibers called tendons.

Muscle building

During exercise, the muscles grow larger. At first, the fibers simply grow fatter. With regular exercise, the body grows new muscle fibers, which means they become stronger. The blood supply improves, too, so the muscles can work longer without tiring.

▶ Fibers in the voluntary muscles move the bones.

On demand

There are 640 voluntary muscles on the skeleton. The brain can only consciously control combinations that work together, rather than individual muscles. The longest is the sartorius muscle at the front of the thigh, while the biggest is the gluteus maximus in the buttocks.

STRONG Structure

Bones give the body a strong, rigid, light framework. Bone can stand being squeezed twice as much as granite and stretched four times as much as concrete. Yet it's so light that bone accounts for barely 14 percent of the body's weight.

A lasting framework

The skeleton is made of 206 bones. As living tissue, the bones are constantly replenished with new cells that grow in the bone's center, called the marrow. The skeleton is the only body part that survives long after death.

THE HAND AND WRIST HAVE ABOUT 30 SMALL JOINTS.

Living bones

Bones are packed with living cells called osteocytes. Each osteocyte sits in a little pocket called a lacuna, and is constantly washed in blood. Some, called osteoblasts, make new bone. Others, called osteoclasts, break down the old, worn-out bone. The soft spongy center or "marrow" of bone produces new blood cells.

The tiniest bone is in **the ear**. It's called the stirrup bone and is only 3 mm long.

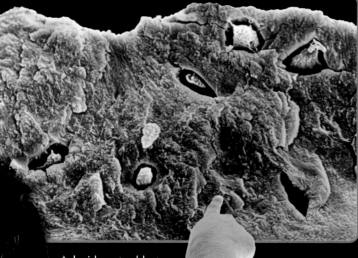

▲ Inside osteoblast cells, lumps of calcium salts crystallize to make hard bone.

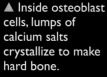

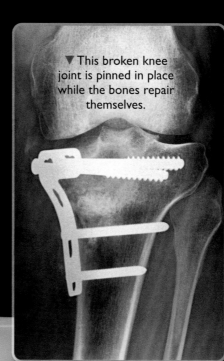

▼ This broken knee joint is pinned in place while the bones repair themselves.

Broken bones

Bones are strong, but they can break or "fracture." Most fractures heal—the body stems any bleeding, then gradually fills the gap with osteoblasts, which weave new bone across the break. The break may need to be straightened and the bone held in place with pins or a plaster cast to ensure it repairs in the right way.

The **appendicular skeleton** is the 126 bones that hang off the axial skeleton—the shoulders, arms and hands, and hips, legs, and feet.

The **axial skeleton** is the 80 bones of the upper body, including the skull, spine, ribs, and breastbone.

Bone strength

Bones are an engineering triumph. Being hollow makes them light. Their strength comes from a combination of flexible collagen fibers and honeycomb struts called trabeculae. Trabeculae are thin but perfectly angled to resist stresses.

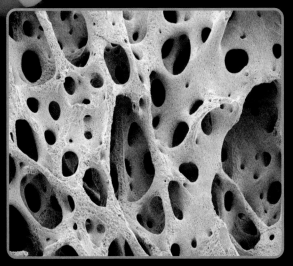

◀ The network of trabeculae inside a bone make it both strong and light.

WITH EVERY STEP, THE THIGH BONE BEARS A CRUNCHING PRESSURE OF 450 LB PER SQ IN (31 KG PER SQ CM).

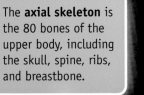

▼ The human foot has 26 bones and 33 joints for balance and mobility.

Mobile skeleton

The skeleton is strong and rigid, yet can bend. It's made of lots of separate bones that are linked by flexible joints. At the joints, bones are held together by fibers called ligaments and cushioned by smooth, rubbery cartilage.

ALIEN INVADERS

You might think you're clean, but you're actually a zoo of microscopic bugs. Living inside your guts are up to 1,000 different species of bacteria—and a similar number are encamped on your skin. Then there are fungi and viruses, mosquitoes, fleas, bedbugs, blackflies, botflies, lice, leeches, ticks, mites, and worms...

Very lice

The head louse (*plural lice*) is a tiny insect that has made human hair its only home for thousands of years. Lice are just big enough to see with the naked eye. They cannot fly, and spend all their lives crawling through their host's hair sucking tiny amounts of blood from the scalp.

Mite have

Your feet, wrists, genitals, and the roots of your hairs are home to a little bug—the follicle mite. Mites are related to spiders, but they are so small, even as adults (less than 0.25 mm long), that you can't see them with the naked eye.

◀ These tiny mites live in the roots of human eyelashes.

◀ The head louse spends its entire life in human hair.

RESISTANCE IS FUTILE!

IN 1991, DOCTORS REMOVED A 37-FT- (11-M-) LONG TAPEWORM FROM AMERICAN SALLY MAE WALLACE'S GUT.

Got you taped

In some parts of the world, people who have eaten uncooked meat end up with flat, ribbonlike tapeworms living in their gut. These worms settle in and feed off the food the infected person eats, soon making their host ill. They are so flat and the human guts are so long that they can grow to more than 30 ft (9 m) in length!

▲ The head of a tapeworm has suckers for gripping the inside of the gut.

Coli wobbles

About 0.1 percent of the bacteria living in the gut belongs to the strain *Escherichia coli*. Most *E coli* are harmless, but occasionally they can make you ill with food poisoning. They enter the body on unwashed vegetables or in uncooked meat, then multiply and release floods of toxins in the intestines.

▼ Under UV light, bacteria can be seen on the hands.

▲ *E coli* bacteria live in your gut and supply you with vitamins K2 and B1.

Skin bugs

A powerful microscope reveals your skin is absolutely crawling with tiny bacteria. Many are Actinobacteria, which are also common in soil. Although there are many billions of bacteria living on your skin, they are so small, their combined volume is no bigger than a pea.

MILLIONS ARE COMING!

BODY DEFENDERS!

THE BODY OFTEN COMES UNDER ATTACK FROM DISEASE-CAUSING BACTERIA, VIRUSES, AND OTHER GERMS. TO DEFEND AGAINST THESE ONSLAUGHTS, THE BODY IS ARMED WITH AN AMAZING SERIES OF BIOLOGICAL WEAPONS, KNOWN AS... THE IMMUNE SYSTEM.

I'M GOING TO MAKE YOU SUFFER!

Bacteria cause diseases such as whooping cough, tetanus, and typhoid.

THE VILLAINS

Germs cause illness when they invade or "infect" the body and multiply.

Viruses are tiny and cause diseases such as colds, flu, mumps, rabies, and AIDS.

Sometimes, germs beat the outer defenses and get inside the body to start their nasty work.

OUTER DEFENSE

Like a fortress, the body has lots of barriers and booby traps to stop germs getting in. The first barrier is the skin.

KEEP OUT!

WE'RE IN! TIME TO CAUSE SOME DAMAGE...

When germs sneak in, they get bogged down in slimy mucus in the nose and lungs—and blasted out with a sneeze or cough. The stomach vomits germs out!

Germs make you feel ill with the toxins they release. Plus, the body's battle against these intruders can cause fever, aching joints, and inflammation. It's time for the inner defenses to get ready...

FIRST INNER DEFENSE

Floods of little "complement" proteins mob the intruding germs.

WHAT?!?

They send out an alarm to the body, which causes soreness and inflammation.

SEND IN THE SPECIALS!

PHAGOCYTES

Troops of "special forces" are called in—the phagocytes. There are three types of phagocyte—granulocytes, dendritic cells, and macrophages.

MACROPHAGE

GRANULOCYTE

DENDRITIC CELL

Phagocyte means "eating cell," and they take no prisoners, simply swallowing the invading germs whole.

MMM, TASTY!

OH DEAR...

Sometimes germs multiply and overwhelm the first defenses. More help is needed, urgently...

Battle casualties are swept through the body's drains—the lymphatic system.

THIS IS VERY DRAINING...

SECOND INNER DEFENSE

At lymph nodes, white blood cells called lymphocytes get to work. They identify the enemy and get ready to unleash an all-out defense.

Lymphocytes called T-helpers look for each germ's unique identity tag or "antigen," found on its surface. They search for traces of antigen on phagocytes that have already been dining on germs.

I KNOW WHAT YOU'VE BEEN EATING!

When the T-helpers have identified the antigens, they alert the B lymphocytes. There's a different B lymphocyte for every kind of germ.

GET READY!

The B lymphocytes make floods of identifying labels called antibodies for their chosen antigen. The antibodies then latch on to the antigens of invading germs.

EAT ME! EAT ME! EAT ME! EAT ME!

The phagocytes detect the antibodies, which make their germ-dinner supertasty.

I'M A GONER!

Finally, the phagocytes devour all the germs and the body starts to recover.

Other germs such as viruses hide inside cells...

YOUR NUMBER'S UP!

They are targeted by lymphocytes called killer T cells, which simply kill the affected cell.

WE'RE READY FOR YOU!
Once it's been through an infection, the immune system is primed with the right antibodies to defend against a future attack. That's why the body rarely gets ill from the same infection twice.

Repair
and
Rebuild

The body is remarkably good at shielding itself against harm and repairing any damage. Sometimes, though, it needs medical help. Vaccines arm the body's immune system against future infections, antibiotic drugs kill many disease-causing bacteria, and surgery corrects defects.

▶ This titanium knee joint (red) replaced a knee destroyed by bone disease.

New joints

Bones are tough, but can be damaged, especially at the joints. With the aid of special materials such as titanium, surgeons can remove a damaged joint and replace it with an artificial one that lasts for ten years. By using a computer to visualize the replacement, it is always a perfect match.

▼ Scottish firefighter Ian Reid, who lost his hand in an accident, has a bionic replacement that can grip as tightly as a real hand.

Bionic bodies

Artificial hands and limbs respond to nerve signals directly from the brain. Therefore a person only has to think to control the tiny electric motors that make a bionic, or prosthetic, hand move. Bionics are used to replace lost or irreversibly damaged hands or limbs. In the future, soldiers may have extra bionics to give them "super powers."

ADD-ON POWERED LIMBS COULD ENABLE A SOLDIER TO RUN UP A HILL CARRYING MORE THAN 650 LB (300 KG).

▶ This replacement bladder was grown on a mold from stem cells in just five weeks.

Organ growing

Scientists can now make replacement body parts in the laboratory. They start with special "stem" cells that can grow into any kind of cell. The stem cells form into the right shape on a special mold of microfibers. Once the new organ has grown, the mold dissolves and the organ can be transplanted into the body.

Disease control

Many deadly diseases have been brought under control using vaccination. This is where the body is infected with a weakened or "dead" version of a germ. In response, the body builds up antibodies, so it is ready to fight back if ever exposed to the real disease.

New cells for old

Stem cells can grow into almost any other kind of cell. In the future, stem cells may be produced to make cells that replace faulty ones. Scientists may then be able to treat anything from cancer to multiple sclerosis, blindness, and even baldness.

◀ Faulty organs might be repaired by using stem cells from embryos such as this three-day-old human embryo.

▲ Smallpox caused about 400 million deaths during the 20th century. It was finally eradicated by vaccination in the 1970s.

IN 2011, A MAN WAS GIVEN A NEW THROAT GROWN FROM STEM CELLS—THE FIRST LAB-GROWN REPLACEMENT ORGAN.

CHEMICAL Messengers

How does the body know when to grow and by how much? How does it cope with stress? How does it keep thousands of substances in the right balance? The complex task of controlling the body is managed by an extraordinary system of chemicals called hormones.

Hormones and glands

Hormones are chemicals that have particular effects on certain cells. "Endocrine" glands release tiny drops of hormone into the blood to spread around the body. Each gland releases its own type of hormone, and each hormone has a special task.

▶ Thyroglobulin (shown in orange) makes thyroid hormones to control the body's energy usage.

THE PITUITARY GLAND WEIGHS LESS THAN ONE GRAM. BUT IT IS ONE OF THE MOST IMPORTANT ORGANS IN THE BODY.

Stop & Go

Hormones work automatically using clever "feedback" systems. The liver supplies the blood with the energy chemical glucose. If blood glucose levels rise too high, the pancreas releases the hormone insulin, which feeds back to the liver, triggering it to stop supplying glucose.

▲ Islets of Langerhans cells in the pancreas release hormones to control sugar levels in the blood.

Grow-faster chemicals

The thyroid gland in the neck and pituitary gland in the brain are no bigger than cherries, but supply vital hormones to make sure the body grows normally. The three thyroid hormones control how fast cells burn energy. The pituitary gland makes the growth hormone, which controls how fast cells grow and multiply.

▼ Too much growth hormone can make the body grow unusually big. Sultan Kösen has the largest handspan in the world at 12 in (30.5 cm) wide.

Adrenaline rush

A sudden scare prepares the body for danger, as it triggers a flood of the hormones adrenaline and noradrenaline. As the hormones rush into the blood, they make the heartbeat faster and stronger. This boosts the blood supply to the muscles to help you run or fight. The blood supply to the skin is restricted, making it go pale and cold. The eyes widen, giving better vision.

▶ During extreme activities, such as bungee jumping, hormones releases for "fight or flight".

ARTIFICALLY MADE STEROID HORMONES CAN BE USED IN INHALERS TO REDUCE THE EFFECTS OF ASTHMA.

Time for change

At a certain age, known as puberty, sex hormones start to be released into the body. A female's ovaries make estrogen and progesterone, which control the menstrual cycle. A male's testes make testosterone, which promotes the production of sperm and creates characteristics such as a deep voice and bigger muscles.

▶ When blood is evaporated, the sex hormone testosterone is left behind as crystals.

speed
MACHINES

Experience the awesome power of acceleration as you hurtle through the adrenaline-fueled world of speed.

◄ The fastest racing motorbikes compete in the MotoGP championship. Using great skill and accuracy, the riders are able to position their bikes only inches from each other at high speed.

RAIL Stars

High-speed trains with a top speed of up to 200 mph (320 km/h), or even faster, whisk passengers from city to city in Europe and the Far East. These sleek, streamlined electric trains run on special tracks so they don't need to slow down for other trains or tight bends.

AGV
FASTEST WHEELED TRAIN IN PASSENGER SERVICE

Years of service: From 2012
Developed in: France
Top speed: 220 mph (360 km/h)
Capacity: Up to 650 passengers
Train length: Up to 820 ft (250 m)

GOING FASTER

The fastest and most modern high-speed trains in Europe are called AGV (Automotrice à Grande Vitesse). Instead of having a power car at each end of the train, an AGV has electric motors under its whole length, making more room inside for passengers. The AGV can go faster than other trains because it has more efficient motors and a more streamlined shape.

TGV
FASTEST WHEELED TRAIN

Years of service: From 1981
Developed in: France
Top speed: 357 mph (574 km/h)
Capacity: 345—750 passengers
Train length: 657—1,293 ft (200—394 m)

AGV TRAINS CAN MAKE A JOURNEY OF 600 MI (1,000 KM) IN ONLY THREE HOURS.

SUPER TGV

French high-speed trains called TGV normally carry passengers at an average speed of 175 mph (280 km/h), but a specially modified TGV set a world-record speed of 357 mph (574 km/h) on April 3, 2007. This is faster than a racing car at full throttle and it's still the world-record speed for any wheeled train.

SHANGHAI MAGLEV

FASTEST TRAIN IN PASSENGER SERVICE

Years of service: From 2004
Developed in: Germany
Top speed: 268 mph (431 km/h)
Capacity: 450 passengers
Train length: 422 ft (129 m)

FLYING TRAINS

Magnetic levitation trains, or maglevs, are lifted and propelled above the track by powerful magnets in the track and train. As maglevs don't touch the track, there is less friction so they can go very fast. The Shanghai maglev in China is the only high-speed passenger maglev in service. It carries passengers between Shanghai and the city's international airport, a distance of 18.6 mi (30 km), in only seven minutes and 20 seconds.

HARMONY EXPRESS

FASTEST WHEELED TRAIN UNTIL 2011

Years of service: From 2007
Developed in: China
Top speed: 236 mph (380 km/h)
Capacity: Up to 1,200 passengers
Train length: 1,310 ft (399 m)

EXPRESS SERVICE

Within one minute of setting off from Wuhan to Guangzhou, the fastest of China's Harmony Express trains is already traveling at 120 mph (195 km/h). It can carry on accelerating until it reaches more than 186 mph (300 km/h).

JR-MAGLEV MLX01

FASTEST MANNED TRAIN

Years of service: Not in service
   (experimental only)
Developed in: Japan
Top speed: 361 mph (581 km/h)
Capacity: Engineers only
Train length: 3 cars

TEST TRAIN

An experimental maglev in Japan is the world's fastest manned train. It is used for research into high-speed maglevs. The JR-Maglev MLX01 was clocked at 361 mph (581 kph) in 2003. This sleek-looking train was built by the Central Japan Railway Company and the Railway Technical Research Institute in 1996.

THE ABSOLUTE RAIL SPEED RECORD IS HELD BY A ROCKET-POWERED SLED, WHICH REACHED A SPEED OF 6,589 MPH (10,603 KM/H) IN 2008.

SUPERSONIC
in the Skies

The fastest military planes in service today are supersonic—they fly faster than the speed of sound. Immensely powerful jet engines boost them to a top speed of more than 1,500 mph (2,400 km/h).

Thundering boom

When a plane reaches the speed of sound, the air in front of it can't move out of the way fast enough. The air piles up in front of the plane and gets squashed into a high-pressure wall called a shock wave. The shock wave spreads out into the surrounding air. If it reaches the ground, you hear it as a bang—a sonic boom—as it sweeps past.

MACH 1

Sound travels faster in warm air than in cold air. In warm air near the ground, the speed of sound might be 774 mph (1,246 km/h). In cold air high above the ground, where jet planes fly, the speed of sound might be as low as 660 mph (1,062 km/h). Mach 1 is the speed of something moving through air (or a fluid) compared to the speed of sound. A plane flying at Mach 1 is flying at the speed of sound.

A SHOCK WAVE SPREADS OUT FROM THE NOSE OF A SUPERSONIC AIRCRAFT LIKE A BOAT'S BOW WAVE.

X PLANES
SUPERSONIC

X-planes are a series of experimental aircraft built since the 1940s to test new flight technologies. The first problem the X-planes were put to work on was how to fly faster than the speed of sound. It took 50 flights in nearly two years to make the first supersonic flight.

1947 Chuck Yeager makes history by piloting the rocket-powered X-1 through the sound barrier.

X-1

1951 The X-5 can change the angle of its wings to study its effect on a plane's speed.

X-5

MAX SPEED: **MACH 1** **MACH 0.95**

Roasting reheat

Some fighters are boosted to supersonic speed using reheat—burning extra fuel in the engine exhaust to give the plane an additional push. Reheat is also used to supply more power for takeoff, but it uses up fuel very quickly. Planes such as the F-22 Raptor can fly at supersonic speeds without having to use reheat. This is called supercruise.

◀ Burning extra fuel to go supersonic gives a fighter a fiery trail.

Making clouds

Shock waves are invisible, but sometimes the weather conditions are just right for them to show up. When a supersonic plane hurtles through moist air, a cloud may form behind the shock wave. It's called a vapor cone. Rockets can cause the same effect, so if you see a rocket being launched, watch carefully and you might see a vapor cone forming around it as it soars through the air on its way into space.

▶ A vapor cone is visible behind this fighter aircraft as it passes through the sound barrier.

▼ The Eurofighter has tiny wings called canards on its nose to enable it to maneuver faster.

Flying ducks

For a supersonic fighter, being able to turn, dive, and climb quickly is just as important as its top speed. Fast maneuvers help a pilot to track a target or to escape from danger quickly. Some fighters have tiny wings called canards (French for "duck") on their nose. Tilting the canards lets the plane perform lightning-fast maneuvers.

X-1A

1953 The X-1A is built to study flight at speeds faster than twice the speed of sound.

MACH 2.4

X-2

1954 The X-2 uses more advanced swept-back wings to try to push its speed faster.

MACH 3.1

X-1E

1955 Based on the X-1, the tiny-winged X-1E is the last of the first X-plane series.

MACH 2.24

AWESOME
Hyperplanes

Aircraft that fly faster than the speed of sound are supersonic, but aircraft that fly faster than five times the speed of sound are *hyper*sonic. Experimental hypersonic aircraft are already being built and tested. A hypersonic airliner would be able to carry passengers from New York, U.S., to Tokyo, Japan, in two hours—a flight that takes about 12 hours today.

▶ Boeing's X-51A is designed to test scramjet engines flying at 3,600 mph (5,800 km/h) or more.

SCRAMJETS

Scramjet engine

Hypersonic aircraft need special engines because ordinary jet engines don't work at such high speeds. They are powered by rockets or jet engines called scramjets. A scramjet engine has no moving parts. Air flows into the engine and is squashed. Then burning fuel makes the air expand and rush out of the engine as a fast jet, propelling the aircraft forward at high speed.

Heat given out

Super boost

On May 26, 2010, an unmanned experimental aircraft called the Boeing X-51A Waverider was dropped from a B-52 bomber. Its rocket engine fired and boosted it to Mach 4.5. Then its scramjet engine started and accelerated it to Mach 5.

◀ Colors are used to show the temperature of the X-43A at Mach 7. Red is the hottest.

PLANES
HYPERSONIC

The X-15 rocket plane was the first manned hypersonic aircraft. It made 199 test flights between 1959 and 1968, reaching a maximum speed of nearly seven times the speed of sound. The X-43A and X-51A are unmanned aircraft, built to test the scramjet engines that will power future hypersonic aircraft.

1951 The pilotless X-7 was an early testbed for hypersonic engines.

X-7

1967 One of the most awesome hyperplanes, the X-15 carried a pilot, propelling Captain William Knight to 4,520 mph (7,275 km/h).

X-15

MAX SPEED: **MACH 4.3**   **MACH 6.7**

The X-43A set a speed record of 7,546 mph (12,144 km/h).

The world airspeed record for an aircraft powered by a jet engine is held by NASA's X-43A. This 12-ft- (3.7-m-) long unmanned vehicle is an experimental hypersonic aircraft. In a test flight on November 16, 2004, it reached a speed of almost ten times the speed of sound.

Faster and further

Hypersonic airliners are already being designed and will be able to fly passengers to the other side on the world in a fraction of the time taken today. They will need very advanced engines that work like ordinary jet engines when the plane takes off, but change to scramjets when the plane accelerates to its hypersonic cruising speed.

▲ The A2 is a future hypersonic airliner designed to fly 300 passengers from western Europe to Australia in less than five hours—a flight that takes 20 hours today.

00:00:00

X-51A IS DESIGNED TO FLY MORE THAN SIX TIMES FASTER THAN A JET AIRLINER.

Speed MACHINES

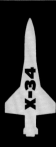

2000 Designed to deliver cargo to other spacecraft, the X-34 project was canceled before the craft flew.

X-34

MACH 8.0

2004 The tiny X-43A is an unmanned scramjet testbed, launched from the nose of a winged booster rocket. Its top speed of Mach 9.8 is 7,546 mph (12,144 km/h)!

X-43A

MACH 9.8

2010 The flight of X-51A featured the longest scramjet engine run to date —just 140 seconds!

X-51A

MACH 5.0

Top TAKEOFF

Planes are able to take off only if they move through the air fast enough. An airliner has to accelerate to at least 150 mph (240 km/h) before its wings create enough lift to cause the plane to defy gravity and leave the ground.

▶ Concorde's mighty jet engines powered the plane to a top speed of more than 1,300 mph (2,100 km/h).

The need for speed

The supersonic airliner Concorde had to go much faster than other airliners before it could take off. Its wings were built for flying at twice the speed of sound, so they didn't produce much lift at lower speeds. Concorde had to reach 225 mph (360 km/h) before its slender wings generated enough upward force for takeoff.

▼ A navy pilot prepares to be launched along the deck and into the air by catapult.

Elastic fantastic

An aircraft carrier has a runway, but it isn't long enough for modern fighter jets to reach takeoff speed. Jets have to be hurled along the deck by a powerful catapult so they're going fast enough to fly when they reach the end. The catapult can boost a 47,000-lb (21-ton) plane from zero to 165 mph (265 km/h) in only two seconds.

Air drop

Some of the fastest aircraft can't take off under their own power. Instead, they are carried into the air by another aircraft. SpaceShipOne was a rocket plane carried aloft by an aircraft called White Knight. At a height of 50,000 ft (15,240 m), White Knight dropped SpaceShipOne, which then fired its rocket and soared away. Being launched in the air like this saved weight and enabled SpaceShipOne to fly faster and higher.

▼ White Knight was specially designed to take off with the SpaceShipOne rocket plane hanging beneath it.

White Knight

SpaceShipOne

THE CATAPULTS THAT LAUNCH NAVY PLANES FROM AIRCRAFT CARRIERS ARE POWERED BY HIGH-PRESSURE STEAM.

THE AIRBUS A380 WEIGHS AS MUCH AS 165 ELEPHANTS.

GIANT flyer

The enormous Airbus A380 is the world's biggest airliner. Its massive wings cover enough space to park 140 cars. This huge airliner accelerates to a speed of 170 mph (280 km/h) on the ground before its wings are able lift the 1.25-million-lb (625-ton) aircraft into the air.

▼ The shape and enormous size of the A380 airliner's wings enable it to take off at the same speed as much smaller, lighter planes.

▶ A racing boat can take off if it bounces off a wave and air rushes underneath, pushing it upward.

Keep it down

The fastest cars and boats are sometimes in danger of taking off. In 1983, Richard Noble set a land speed record of 633 mph (1,018 km/h) in his jet-powered car, *Thrust 2*. If he'd gone just 7 mph (11 km/h) faster, *Thrust 2* would have taken off!

Space
SPEEDERS

What goes up must come down... unless it's a spacecraft. Gravity normally pulls everything down to Earth, but if something travels fast enough, it goes into orbit or heads out toward the Moon or planets. The closer an orbiting spacecraft is to Earth, the faster it has to travel to stay in orbit.

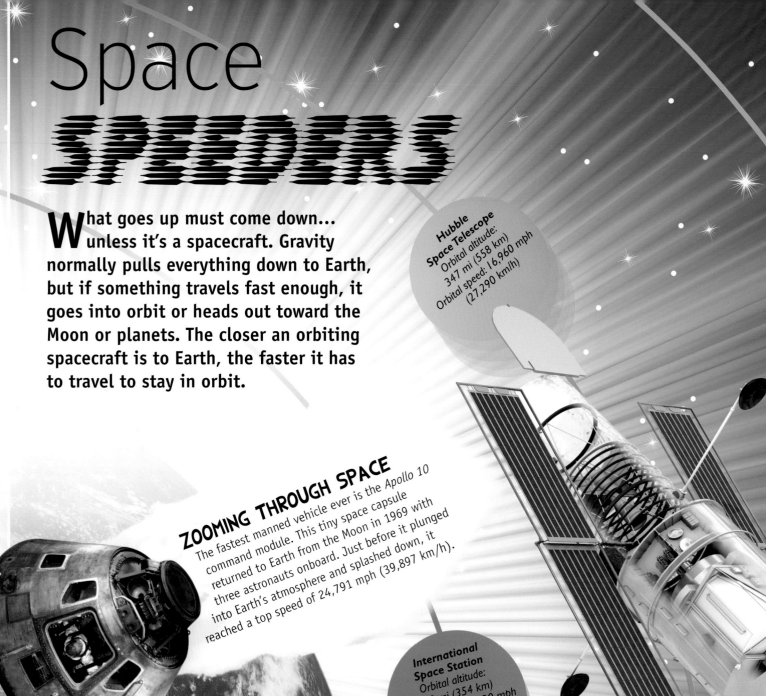

Hubble Space Telescope
Orbital altitude: 347 mi (558 km)
Orbital speed: 16,960 mph (27,290 km/h)

ZOOMING THROUGH SPACE

The fastest manned vehicle ever is the Apollo 10 command module. This tiny space capsule returned to Earth from the Moon in 1969 with three astronauts onboard. Just before it plunged into Earth's atmosphere and splashed down, it reached a top speed of 24,791 mph (39,897 km/h).

International Space Station
Orbital altitude: 220 mi (354 km)
Orbital speed: 17,220 mph (27,720 km/h)

Space flyer

The International Space Station is gradually slowed down by the thin wisps of atmosphere it flies through, which causes it to lose height. It has to be moved back up to a higher orbit several times a year by firing its own rocket engines or those of a visiting spacecraft.

Eye in the sky

The Hubble Space Telescope has completed one orbit of Earth every 97 minutes since its launch in 1990. From its vantage point above the cloudy atmosphere, Hubble's cameras and other instruments have a clear view of stars and galaxies.

THE INTERNATIONAL SPACE STATION ORBITS THE WORLD SO FAST THAT THE ASTRONAUTS ONBOARD SEE 15 SUNRISES IN EVERY 24 HOURS.

GPS navigation satellite
Orbital altitude: 12,550 mi (20,200 km)
Orbital speed: 8,660 mph (13,930 km/h)

SPOT-5 Earth observation satellite
Orbital altitude: 510 mi (820 km)
Orbital speed: 16,651 mph (26,800 km/h)

Meteosat weather satellite
Orbital altitude: 22,370 mi (36,000 km)
Orbital speed: 6,870 mph (11,050 km/h)

Studying Earth

SPOT-5 is an Earth observation satellite. It circles the world from pole to pole, completing an orbit every 101 minutes as Earth spins beneath it. It passes over each part of the planet every 26 days. Launched in 2002, SPOT-5's photographs are used for town planning, studying land use, terrain modeling, agriculture, monitoring natural disasters, and oil and gas exploration.

Where am I?

GPS (Global Positioning System) satellites help travelers to locate their position and calculate the journey to a specific destination. Their orbit is 60 times higher than the International Space Station. GPS began as a military project to enable U.S. nuclear missile submarines to work out precisely where they were in the ocean.

Watching the weather

Meteosat weather satellites monitor Earth's weather systems. Their orbit above the Equator is chosen so that they take 24 hours to circle Earth. As Earth spins once every 24 hours, too, the satellite appears to hover over the same spot. This is called a geostationary orbit.

STRANGE Sailboats

Yachts that are specially built to win races and set speed records don't look like ordinary boats. They are designed to squeeze every possible bit of power out of the wind—skimming across the top of the water or even flying above it.

IN DECEMBER 2008, AT A SPEED OF 59 MPH (95 KM/H), SAILROCKET 1 TOOK OFF, SOMERSAULTED IN MIDAIR, AND CRASHED INTO THE SEA!

▶ Sailrocket 2 will try to beat the world speed sailing record. Its odd shape is designed so that both the water and wind forces acting on the boat are perfectly balanced.

Rocket boat

One of the strangest-looking, high-speed yachts is a record-breaker called *Sailrocket 2*. Its sail stands on a float to one side of the boat's hull. The sail is rigid, like a plane's wing standing on end. It is perfectly shaped to propel the yacht at high speed in strong winds. The pilot sits in a tiny cockpit at one end of the hull.

▲ The catamaran Alinghi 5 chases the trimaran USA-17 in a thrilling dash to the finish line. The masts of these giant racing yachts stand nearly 200 ft (60 m) high.

▲ International Moths are tricky to sail. Sailors use their weight to keep the tiny boats balanced.

Underwater wings

International Moths are small, one-person sailing boats just over 10 ft (3 m) long. Each boat's ultralight hull weighs only 20 lb (10 kg). Like the giant hydrofoil yacht, *Hydroptère*, International Moths have underwater wings. When their hulls rise out of the water—which doubles their speed—they sail along silently. The world record speed for an International Moth is 35.3 mph (56.9 km/h), set by Rob Gough during a training session on May 2, 2010, near Hobart, Tasmania.

Two hulls or three?

Most boats have one hull—the part of the boat that sits in the water. The fastest racing yachts have two or even three hulls. Two or three slender hulls cut through the water faster than one large hull. A two-hulled yacht is called a catamaran and a three-huller is known as a trimaran. In the hands of an expert crew, a racing yacht can reach a top speed of more than 35 mph (55 km/h).

▶ On September 4, 2009, *Hydroptère* set a world record yacht speed of 59 mph (95 km/h).

French flyer

The record-breaking yacht *Hydroptère* looks like an ordinary racing yacht until it starts picking up speed. It rises higher and higher until its hull is out of the water altogether. The secret of its amazing performance is a pair of underwater wings called hydrofoils. As they slice through the water, they work like aircraft wings and lift the whole boat. Eventually, only the wings are in the water. As the hull doesn't have to push through the water, *Hydroptère* can reach high speeds.

Power and SPRAY

Powerboats can speed through water as fast as racing cars move on land. All sorts and sizes of powerboats race against each other, from tiny one-person craft to mighty ocean-going vessels. The boats are divided into types, or classes, each with its own design rules. When the starting gun is fired, their spinning propellers turn the water into frothy, white foam as they accelerate to awesome speeds.

Ocean racers

Offshore powerboat racers can plow through the waves at astonishing speeds. Class 1 boats are the fastest. These racing machines are catamarans up to 50 ft (15 m) long and weighing about 5.5 tons (5 tons). Their twin engines can power them through the waves at up to 150 mph (240 km/h).

▶ The super-streamlined hulls of these offshore powerboats slice across the wave tops as they vie for a top position during a thrilling race.

RACING BOATS OFTEN HAVE PROPELLERS AT THE WATER'S SURFACE, CALLED SURFACE-PIERCING PROPELLERS.

MOST BOATS AND SHIPS ARE MOVED THROUGH THE WATER BY PROPELLERS UNDERNEATH THE VESSEL.

WITH ONLY HALF OF EACH PROPELLER UNDERWATER, THEY ENABLE A BOAT TO GO UP TO 30 PERCENT FASTER THAN THOSE WITH UNDERWATER PROPELLERS.

Power planing

Hydroplanes are small, single-engine racing boats that skim across the surface of the water instead of pushing through it. As they speed up, they rise higher until they're sitting on top of the water. This is called planing. When a hydroplane is planing, it touches the water at only three small points—two floats called sponsons at the front and the propeller at the back.

▲ Hydroplanes can exceed 100 mph (160 km/h) and a few have topped 200 mph (320 km/h) on a straight course.

Grand Prix of the Sea

Powerboat Grand Prix of the Sea (GPS) is the fastest-growing type of international powerboat racing. There are two classes of GPS boats—Evolution and Supersport. Evolution boats are specially built for racing. They're about 43 ft (13 m) long and weigh as much as 15,400 lb (7.7 tons). Supersport boats are the same as boats that anyone can buy. All GPS boats are twin-engine monohulls, crewed by at least two people—a pilot who steers the boat and someone who controls the engine power.

EACH OF A CLASS 1 RACING POWERBOAT'S TWO ENGINES IS FOUR OR FIVE TIMES BIGGER THAN A FAMILY CAR ENGINE.

▲ Powerboat GPS racing boats can reach top speeds of 125 mph (200 km/h).

PUSHING
the Limit

Sports scientists are constantly looking for ways to make athletes go faster within the rules of their sports. In their quest to win races and set records, they make use of the latest inventions, advances in technology, and cutting-edge materials to push the human body to new limits.

Carbon magic

Cyclists who compete at the highest level ride the most advanced bicycles. Olympic bikes are made of an ultralightweight material called carbon fiber. To save even more weight, there are no brakes or gears, meaning the whole bike can weigh less than 15 lb (7 kg).

▲ High-tech swimsuits enable swimmers, such as American Michael Phelps, to glide through water faster.

A second skin

To increase a swimmer's speed, scientists looked to the animal world for inspiration. Sharks are efficient swimmers because their skin is covered with tiny toothlike points called denticles, making it easier for water to flow round the body. Scientists created swimsuits that mimic shark skin and added elastic panels to streamline the swimmer's body. Of the 25 swimming world records broken at the Beijing Olympics in 2008, 23 were by swimmers wearing these high-tech suits.

THE CARBON FIBER MATERIAL THAT RACING BIKES ARE MADE OF IS UP TO TEN TIMES STRONGER AND FOUR TIMES LIGHTER THAN STEEL.

▲ An Olympic racing bike has spokeless disk wheels to reduce air resistance or drag.

▼ Wearing a pointed helmet cuts the speed-sapping drag caused by a cyclist's head by two percent.

Mad hatters

The pointed helmet worn by a track cyclist gives the rider's head the most aerodynamic shape to go as fast as possible. It reduces air resistance and lets the rider gain a fraction of a second on every lap of the track.

MANUFACTURERS USE THE STRONGEST MATERIALS AND FIBERS TO MAKE RUNNING SHOES SO LIGHT AND THIN THAT THE RUNNER FEELS ALMOST BAREFOOT.

▼ Blades cleverly mimic the action of human legs, even though they have no moving parts or joints.

Bending blades

Using clever technology, disabled athletes can run as fast as the best able-bodied athletes by wearing carbon fiber "legs" called blades. When a runner takes a step, the body's weight bends the blade and the blade stores the energy produced. As the runner lifts his foot to take the next step, the blade springs back and releases its energy, enabling the runner to move quickly.

Speedy Shapes

The wedge-shaped Italdesign Quaranta is a three-seat, 155-mph (250-km/h) prototype of a future road car.

The shape of a racer or record-breaker is as important as its engine power, and is vital for reaching top speed. The wrong shape catches and stirs up the air, slowing down the vehicle. The right shape lets air slide around the vehicle as quickly and easily as possible without slowing it down.

Virtual world

A lot of vehicle testing is done without using models or wind tunnels. Computers are programmed with a vehicle's size and shape. Then the computer calculates how air would flow around the vehicle. This lets designers check new designs quickly without having to wait for models to be made or wind tunnel tests to be carried out.

A supercomputer simulates the way air flows around a new car. Colors are added to show changes in air pressure.

▼ With an ultrasmooth body and a large area of solar cells on top, some solar-powered racing cars can reach a top speed of 75 mph (120 km/h).

Solar speeders

Air resistance eats up engine power, so shape is especially important for cars that have very little driving force. The electric cars that compete in the World Solar Challenge, a 1,860-mi (3,000-km) race across Australia, are powered by sunlight. The cars are covered with solar cells that change light into electricity. Their body shape is carefully designed to cause the least air resistance.

Shape up

The fastest cars have a sleek, space-age shape because this causes the least drag, enabling them to reach incredible speeds. These cars are usually very low at the front, with a gently curving top. Their streamlined shape, smooth surface, and gentle curves deflect air smoothly around the car.

Blowing a gale

It's important to know what happens to a vehicle when it moves through the air at high speed. Designers use wind tunnels to study this. The vehicle, or a model of it, is held still inside the tunnel and air is blown round it. The vehicle or model is covered with sensors that measure the forces acting on it. The wind is produced by one or more aircraft engines.

▶ The world's biggest wind tunnels can fit full-size vehicles inside and test them in hurricane-force winds.

THE SCIENTIFIC STUDY OF THE WAY AIR FLOWS AROUND OBJECTS IS CALLED AERODYNAMICS.

Rocketing streamliners

Motorcycles that are built specially for setting new speed records are called streamliners and look more like rockets on wheels than motorbikes. The rider lies down on top of the bike inside the slender shell. The fastest motorcycle streamliners can reach speeds in excess of 300 mph (480 km/h).

▲ The Top 1 Ack Attack streamliner set a world-record motorcycle speed of 376 mph (605 km/h) on September 25, 2010.

PARTS UNLIMITED

The Right FORMULA

The Formula 1 world championship is the most popular international motorsport in the world. The cars are engineering and design marvels—half the weight of ordinary family cars, but five times more powerful. As they scythe through the air, their "wings" and body shape create a downforce that sticks them to the track, enabling them to corner—fast.

FIRE!

Each car has an automatic fire extinguisher system that sprays foam all over the chassis and engine if a fire breaks out. The drivers also wear fireproof suits, which can protect them from flames as hot as 1,550°F (840°C) for 11 seconds—long enough for help to arrive.

GAME OVER!

< SELECT CAR >

TIRES—designed to last for only one race, or about 185 mi (300 km), compared to more than 25,000 mi (40,000 km) for ordinary car tires

< MATERIALS >   < CARBON FIBER >

Designers make use of the latest materials to produce an F1 car that is light, yet strong. The car's main frame, or chassis, its body, and many of its smaller parts are made of carbon fiber, a material that is up to ten times stronger than steel and a fraction of its weight.

< SELECT >

Carbon fiber starts off as a flimsy woven mat, but when soaked in resin, it sets hard.

FRONT WING—creates one quarter of the car's downforce

DISK BRAKE—slows or stops the car, using carbon fiber disks that can reach a temperature of 2,200°F (1,200°C)

SURVIVAL CELL—
ultrastrong tub
that surrounds the
driver and provides
protection in an
accident

<<<<< AIR SCOOP—feeds
air into the engine

REAR WING—
creates most of
the car's
downforce

REAR WHEELS—driven
by the engine, they
transfer the engine's >>>>>
enormous power to
the race track

<<<<< ENGINE—2.4–l V8 powerplant,
weighing about 200 lb (95 kg)—
half the weight of an
ordinary V8 car engine

< SAFETY >

< HELMET >

A driver's most important
piece of safety equipment is
his helmet. It is made of
about 20 layers of different
materials—some for strength,
others for fire protection. The
visor is tested by firing
projectiles at it at 310 mph
(500 km/h).

▶ Helmets have been compulsory
in Formula I since 1953.

< HANS
DEVICE >

In a high-speed
accident, a racing
driver's head can be
forced forward so fast
that it breaks his neck.
To stop this from
happening, racing
drivers wear a HANS
(Head And Neck
Support) device.

< SELECT >

START

133

SLEEK Supercars

Fast, powerful, expensive—supercars combine blistering performance with space-age styling. Not only are they as low-slung and streamlined as a racing car, they also have the acceleration to match. Supercars are made only in small numbers by manufacturers including Ferrari, Lamborghini, Porsche, Koenigsegg, Pagani, and Bugatti.

DODGE VIPER

The first thing to notice about a Dodge Viper is its long hood. It covers a massive 8.4-l engine, giving this American supercar a top speed of more than 200 mph (320 km/h). The ten-cylinder engine was developed from a truck engine, but modified to make it lighter and more powerful for use in a sports car.

ENGINE
8.4-l V10;
600 horsepower

0–60 MPH
3.9 sec

TOP SPEED
202 mph (325 km/h)

PRICE
$91,955 (£56,595)

ENZO FERRARI

This Italian car manufacturer has been producing some of the world's fastest racing cars and most desirable sports cars for more than 50 years. The Enzo Ferrari supercar was designed and built using technology from Ferrari's Formula 1 racing cars. All 349 Enzo Ferrari supercars were sold before they were even made. Later, another 51 cars were built to bring the total production to 400 cars. The 400th car was auctioned for charity.

ENGINE
6.0-l V12;
660 horsepower

0–60 MPH
3.65 sec

TOP SPEED
217 mph (350 km/h)

PRICE
$1 million
(£615,400)

THE "AFFORDABLE" SUPERCAR

German car manufacturer Porsche is world-famous for its high-performance sports cars. The Porsche Cayman is powered by a 2.9-l, 265-horsepower engine, giving it a top speed of 165 mph (265 km/h). The engine is in the middle of the car, behind the driver, making the car very stable. This small, lightweight, sporty supercar comes with a price tag of $51,900 (£32,855).

BUGATTI VEYRON

The Bugatti Veyron is the world's fastest production car. The Super Sport model set a world-record speed of 268 mph (431 km/h) on July 3, 2010. Designed for high-speed driving, when it reaches 140 mph (220 km/h), the Veyron automatically lowers itself closer to the ground. At the same time, a wing and spoiler pop up at the back of the car. Air flowing over them help to hold the car down on the road.

ENGINE
8.0-l W16;
1,200 horsepower

0–60 MPH
2.5 sec

TOP SPEED
258 mph
(415 km/h)

PRICE
$2.4 million
(£1.5 million)

LAMBORGHINI

Most cars have two wheels powered by the engine, but all four of the Lamborghini Gallardo's wheels are powered to give improved grip and control. To save weight, the Gallardo's body is made of aluminum instead of steel. Large air intakes under its nose help to keep the powerful mid-mounted engine cool.

ENGINE
5.2-l V10;
560 horsepower

0–60 MPH
3.7 sec

TOP SPEED
202 mph (325 km/h)

PRICE
$220,000 (£139,000)

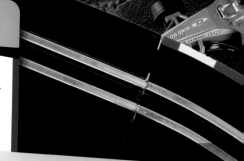

A race between different cars, bikes, boats, and planes—which would win? Would it be the fastest car, the most powerful dragster, or the most maneuverable motorbike? Or would a plane or boat cross the finish line first? Which would be the Ultimate Winner?

UR

ULTIMATE RACE

SPEED MACHINES

NASCAR

NASCAR racing cars look like souped-up production cars, but are individually handbuilt for racing on road circuits and racing ovals.

Top Speed	200 mph (320 km/h)
Acceleration	Very good
Power	800 hp
Endurance	500 mi (805 km/h)
Maneuverability	Moderate

SUPERBIKE

Superbikes are modified production motorcycles, chosen so that fans of the sport can see bikes similar to their own competing on the race track.

Top Speed	205 mph (330 km/h)
Acceleration	Excellent
Power	215 hp
Endurance	68 mi (110 km)
Maneuverability	Excellent

RED BULL RACING PLANE

The aircraft that take part in the Red Bull Air Race World Championship are small, lightweight, highly maneuverable planes designed for aerobatics and racing.

Top Speed	265 mph (426 km/h)
Acceleration	Good
Power	350 hp
Endurance	477 mi (767 km)
Maneuverability	Good

MOTOGP MOTORCYCLE

MotoGP is the leading international motorcycle championship. The bikes are prototypes, more powerful than many cars but just a fraction of a car's weight.

Top Speed	220 mph (350 km/h)
Acceleration	Excellent
Power	240 hp
Endurance	75 mi (120 km)
Maneuverability	Excellent

TOP FUEL DRAGSTER

These extraordinary cars are designed to achieve the maximum acceleration in a straight line. They have minimal steering, which is used only to make small adjustments in direction.

Top Speed	330 mph (530 km/h)
Acceleration	Excellent
Power	7,000 hp
Endurance	0.25 mi (402 m)
Maneuverability	Almost none

FORMULA 1 RACING CAR

F1 cars are specially designed for racing on circuits with left and right turns. Downforce generated by their body and wings enables them to corner at very high speeds.

Top Speed	225 mph (360 km/h)
Acceleration	Excellent
Power	720 hp
Endurance	200 mi (320 km)
Maneuverability	Excellent

GPS RACING POWERBOAT

These racing prototypes and production boats are slender monohulls powered by two engines. The Evolution class prototypes are the fastest of the GPS boats.

Top Speed	125 mph (200 km/h)
Acceleration	Good
Power	725 hp
Endurance	100 mi (160 km)
Maneuverability	Moderate

INDYCAR

IndyCars are a little faster than F1 cars in a straight line, but F1 cars are able to generate more downforce, so they are faster in turns.

Top Speed	240 mph (385 km/h)
Acceleration	Excellent
Power	650 hp
Endurance	500 mi (805 km)
Maneuverability	Good

UNLIMITED HYDROPLANE

These small boats, powered by helicopter engines, reach breathtaking speeds by skating across the top of the water instead of plowing through it.

Top Speed	200 mph (320 km/h)
Acceleration	Good
Power	3,000 hp
Endurance	12.5 mi (20 km)
Maneuverability	Good

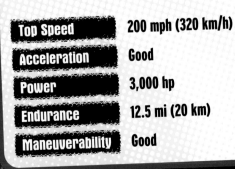

** WINNERS **

Top Speed	Top Fuel Dragster
Acceleration	Top Fuel Dragster
Power	Top Fuel Dragster
Endurance	NASCAR
Maneuverability	Formula 1 racing car

ULTIMATE RACE WINNER:
Formula 1 racing car

Although Top Fuel Dragsters have the best speed, acceleration, and power, F1 cars have the edge with their combination of speed, agility, and endurance. Dragsters can only go in a straight line for 0.25 mi (0.4 km), lasting less than ten seconds. An F1 car can go for hours on a winding track with right and left bends. If you raced a dragster against an F1 car, the dragster would be in the lead at the first corner, then it would either fall over when it tried to turn or it would run out of fuel!

HOT Stuff

Speed and heat go together. When something travels through air very fast, it heats up. The fastest vehicles heat up so much that they would melt if they weren't protected. Airliners that fly up to about twice the speed of sound are made of aluminum. Faster aircraft are made of materials such as titanium that can withstand higher temperatures. Spacecraft that travel even faster need heat shields to protect them.

Shuttle tiles

A heat shield that slowly burns away can be used only once. A different type of heat shield that could be used again and again was developed for the Space Shuttle Orbiter. The hottest parts of the Orbiter reached a temperature of nearly 3,000°F (1,650°C) during reentry—at about 17,000 mph (27,340 km/h) or Mach 25. To protect its aluminum structure, it was covered with heat-resistant tiles and blankets.

▼ The Space Shuttle Orbiter is covered with more than 24,000 tiles. No two tiles are alike—each has a unique shape.

What a scorcher!

When a manned spacecraft reenters Earth's atmosphere, it heats up so much that it becomes a fireball. One way to stop it from melting is to cover the front with a heat shield. The material in an "ablative" heat shield slowly smolders, rather than setting on fire. The new Orion American manned spacecraft currently under construction will use an ablative heat shield to deal with reentry temperatures as high as 5,000°F (2,760°C).

◄ An engineer inspects an Orion spacecraft's heat shield. When this spacecraft returns from the Moon, it will hit Earth's atmosphere at 25,000 mph (40,000 km/h).

The Mars Polar lander's heat shield glows due to friction from Mars' atmosphere.

Landing on Mars

A spacecraft landing on Mars needs a heat shield to save it from burning up as it plunges into the Martian atmosphere. A spacecraft enters the atmosphere at about 12,000 mph (19,300 km/h). The thin atmosphere slows it down and heats it up. Within four minutes, its speed has dropped to 1,000 mph (1,600 km/h) and its heat shield is glowing red-hot. The heat shield has done its job and falls away, leaving the spacecraft to land by parachute.

THE HEAT SHIELD OF A SPACECRAFT ENTERING THE MARTIAN ATMOSPHERE IS HOT ENOUGH TO MELT GOLD.

Space Shuttle tiles were such good insulators that even when they were glowing red-hot in the middle, they could be held safely in the hand.

Cool design

The material chosen for the Space Shuttle's heat shield tiles is an incredibly good insulator. About six percent of it is made of silica, and the rest is air. Heat travels through it very, very slowly. However, the material is very brittle and easily damaged. The Space Shuttle wasn't launched when it was raining, because raindrops could damage the tiles!

SPEEDING UP

Some vehicles accelerate a lot faster than others. One measurement of acceleration is the time a vehicle takes to go from 0 to 60 mph (100 km/h). A family car takes about ten seconds. The jet-propelled land speed record car, *Thrust SSC*, took 2.5 seconds. Dragsters are even faster and reach 60 mph (100 km/h) in less than one second!

Blistering speed

Great acceleration is vital in motor-racing. The car with the best acceleration gets away from the start line first and reaches the first turn in the lead. Formula 1 and IndyCars can go from 0 to 60 mph (100 km/h) in just over two seconds, or about five times faster than a family car.

▲ At full power, a Formula 1 racing car's engine sucks in an amazing 120 gal (450 l) of air every second.

In a flash

The world's fastest pick-up truck, *Flash Fire*, is powered by a 12,000-hp jet engine from a navy plane. The engine thrusts the truck to 60 mph (100 km/h) in just over one second and boosts it to a top speed of 375 mph (603 km/h).

▶ *Flash Fire's* jet engine gets through 60 gal (227 l) of fuel in just ten minutes.

Drag speed

Dragsters accelerate faster than any other car. When the driver of a Top Fuel dragster gets the green light, the car goes from 0 to 60 mph (100 km/h) in half a second. Even faster, a rocket-propelled dragster does this in only one fifth of a second!

Smoke pours from the spinning wheels of a dragster at the beginning of a race.

Dr. John Stapp studied the effects of g-force on the human body in the 1940s and '50s by strapping himself to a rocket sled.

Like a bullet

A handful of street-legal motorbikes can accelerate from 0 to 60 mph (100 km/h) in only 2.5 seconds—almost as fast as a F1 car or IndyCar. The fastest street-legal cars are more than seven times heavier than a motorbike, but they're also more than seven times as powerful, so they too can accelerate from 0 to 60 mph (100 km/h) in about 2.5 seconds.

▼ The Suzuki Hayabusa motorbike accelerates as fast as a racing bike.

AWESOME G-FORCE

People traveling in an accelerating vehicle feel a force acting on them called g-force. The faster the acceleration, the stronger the g-force. Stopping suddenly produces g-force, too. The force of gravity pulling you down to the ground is 1 g. An astronaut feels a force of about 3 g during a launch. A force of 50 g or more is usually fatal, but F1 driver David Purley experienced a momentary force of 180 g during a crash—and survived.

Record BREAKERS

Through history, different types of speed machines have become faster by small amounts as people attempt to develop vehicles that can outdo any previous models. Improvements in performance are usually due to inventions or developments, such as a new engine.

SETTING RECORDS

To set a new land or water speed record, the challenger must make two runs over a measured distance in opposite directions within an hour with an average speed one percent higher than the current record. The absolute air speed record is set over a straight course 9–15 mi (15–25 km) long.

To set an official airspeed record, planes must have air-breathing engines and take off and land under their own power.

AIR

SPEED RECORD

In 1906, only three years after the first plane flew, Alberto Santos-Dumont set the first official airspeed record—25.6 mph (41.3 km/h). As flimsy biplanes were replaced by all-metal monoplanes, and propellers gave way to jet engines, the record rose steadily. The last record was set in 1976 by U.S. Air Force Captain Eldon W. Joersz and Major George T. Morgan flying a Lockheed SR-71 Blackbird spy-plane—2,193 mph (3,529 km/h).

2,193 MPH (3,529 KM/H)

▼ The Blackbird spy-plane could fly at more than three times the speed of sound.

LAND
SPEED RECORD

763 MPH (1,228 KM/H)

The first land speed record was set in 1898 by Frenchman Count Gaston de Chasseloup-Laubat in an electric car. He drove the fastest car in the world at 39 mph (63 km/h). The most famous land speed record cars were the Bluebird cars driven by Malcolm Campbell and, later, his son Donald. In the 1960s, Craig Breedlove set a series of land speed records in cars powered by jet engines. In 1997, a jet-car called *Thrust SSC* driven by Royal Air Force fighter pilot Andy Green set a record of 763 mph (1,228 km/h).

Thrust SSC, powered by two jet-fighter engines, is the first car to set a supersonic land speed record.

BRITISH DRIVER MALCOLM CAMPBELL SET MORE LAND SPEED RECORDS THAN ANYONE ELSE—NINE IN 11 YEARS.

MALCOLM CAMPBELL'S SON, DONALD, IS THE ONLY PERSON EVER TO SET NEW LAND SPEED AND WATER SPEED RECORDS IN THE SAME YEAR—1964.

▲ Donald Campbell set seven world water speed records in *Bluebird K7* between 1955 and 1964.

The current water speed record was set by Ken Warby in a jet-powered boat called *Spirit of Australia* that he designed and built himself. On November 20, 1977, he set off across the Blowering Dam lake in Australia and recorded a speed of 288 mph (464 km/h). He returned to Blowering Dam the next year and raised the record to 317 mph (511 km/h).

▼ *Spirit of Australia* was powered by a 6,000-hp Westinghouse J34 jet engine from a fighter plane.

WATER
SPEED RECORD

317 MPH (511 KM/H)

Number CRUNCHERS

The biggest supercomputers work as fast as a billion people each doing a million calculations every second!

Supercomputers are the world's fastest computers. They tackle the most difficult problems that need huge numbers of calculations done very quickly—only a supercomputer can do the trillions upon trillions of calculations needed to show what happens when two black holes collide with each other in space.

The **first supercomputer** was the CDC 6600, built in 1964. It could do a million calculations in one second. The fastest supercomputers today are about 10,000 million times faster.

The Swiss Federal Institute of Technology is kept warm in winter by water heated by its Aquasar supercomputer.

Computer technology advances so quickly that a desktop PC today is as powerful as a supercomputer was ten years ago.

The speed of the fastest supercomputers is measured in units called **petaflops**—a petaflop is a thousand trillion calculations per second. A trillion is a **million million.**

More than half of the world's top 500 supercomputers are in the U.S.

Every six months, in June and November, a list of the world's 500 fastest computers is published. It's called the **TOP500.**

In October 2010, China's Tianhe-1A supercomputer became the **world's fastest computer** with a speed of **2.5 petaflops,** or 2,500 trillion calculations per second.

Germany's Jugene supercomputer works faster than 50,000 PCs. Its circuit boards fill **72** fridge-sized cabinets.

▼ When Jugene was built in 2007, it was the world's second fastest computer.

Tianhe-1A has the computing power of **175,000** laptops and uses as much electricity as 4,000 homes.

Supercomputers have **doubled** in speed roughly every 14 months since 1993.

Most personal computers use the Microsoft Windows operating system, but nearly all of the world's supercomputers use an operating system called Linux.

In 1996, IBM's Deep Blue became the first supercomputer to win **a chess match** against a world champion chess player, Gary Kasparov.

Supercomputers are able to work so amazingly fast because they have tens of thousands of processors all working at the same time on different parts of a problem—called parallel computing.

Supercomputers are growing in speed and complexity so fast that some scientists think they may become **more intelligent than humans** by about the year 2045.

Supercomputers have to be cooled or they would get hot enough to fry their circuits.

New supercomputers are being built all the time. In June, 2011, a Japanese supercomputer called the K computer reached a speed of **8 petaflops** in tests—more than three times faster than Tianhe-1A.

TOP 10 FASTEST SUPERCOMPUTERS

SUPERCOMPUTER	SPEED*	COUNTRY
1 K	8.162	Japan
2 Tianhe-1A	2.566	China
3 Jaguar	1.759	U.S.
4 Nebulae	1.271	China
5 TSUBAME 2.0	1.192	Japan
6 Cielo	1.110	U.S.
7 Pleiades	1.088	U.S.
8 Hopper	1.054	U.S.
9 Tera 100	1.050	France
10 Roadrunner	1.042	U.S.

* petaflops (thousand million million calculations per second)

The Earth Simulator was a supercomputer built in Japan by NEC in 2002 to study the global climate and climate change. It was the world's fastest supercomputer until 2004.

IBM is building a supercomputer called Sequoia with a computing speed of 20 petaflops—20,000 trillion calculations per second.

GOING UP

If you want to go straight upward as fast as possible, there are lots of ways to choose. You could launch yourself on top of a rocket, zoom up a skyscraper in a high-speed elevator, take a flight in a helicopter, or even hitch a ride on a jet-propelled bedstead!

Space elevator

In the future, you might be able to get to space by taking a ride in an elevator. A cable would extend from the ground to a spacecraft in orbit and an elevator car would climb up the cable to space.

▲ A space elevator would be at least 22,370 mi (36,000 km) tall!

THE FASTEST ELEVATORS CLIMB SO QUICKLY THAT THE CHANGE IN AIR PRESSURE MAKES PASSENGERS' EARS POP.

▲ Two boosters strapped to the sides of an *Atlas V* give the rocket extra power and speed.

Liftoff

The fastest ever rocket to leave Earth is an *Atlas V* that carried the New Horizons space probe on its way to the dwarf planet Pluto. Launched in 2006, it reached a speed of 32,256 mph (51,911 km/h) as it sped away from Earth. The spacecraft was as far away as the Moon in only nine hours.

High rise

Dubai's Burj Khalifa skyscraper is the world's tallest building at 2,717 ft (828 m) high. Its elevators set a new record as the world's fastest in 2010. They whisk people up and down the giant building at up to 40 mph (64 km/h).

IN 1955, THE FIRST ELEVATOR TO HOLD THE TITLE OF THE WORLD'S FASTEST MOVED AT 16 MPH (25.6 KM/H).

High-speed elevators reach the top of Burj Khalifa in less than 60 seconds.

Super chopper

Helicopters can take off straight upward. The fastest helicopter ever built is the Sikorsky X2. A propeller in its tail gives it a top speed of 290 mph (460 km/h). Lessons learned from this experimental super chopper are being used to develop a new high-speed military helicopter.

▲ Sikorsky X2 has two rotors that spin in opposite directions.

Flying bedstead

Apollo astronauts practised landing on the Moon before they did it for real by flying a strange aircraft called the flying bedstead. In the middle, it had a jet engine pointing straight downward.

◄ The flying bedstead was steered by rocket thrusters.

Jet man

How would you like to strap a rocket to your back? In a jetpack, hydrogen peroxide fuel in a tank on the pilot's back is converted into steam. The steam takes up more space than the liquid fuel, so it jets out of two pipes that point downward. The jets push the pilot up into the air. The pilot steers by swiveling the jet pipes.

▼ The pilot can only carry enough fuel for flights of 20–30 seconds.

Thrill SEEKERS

Marvel at the amazing feats of champion risk takers and witness daredevils pushing themselves to the limit.

◄ Swiss pilot Yves Rossy is the first person to fly for a set period of time using a wingsuit. In 2011, he flew across the Grand Canyon, Arizona, U.S.

Taking to THE SKIES

Dropping like a stone from a high-flying aircraft would be a white-knuckle, breathtaking dare for most of us. But for some thrill seekers, ordinary skydiving is just far too dull. Instead, they push risk to the limit, jumping fast and low, from earthbound objects, or in tight formation.

BASE JUMPING IS THE WORLD'S MOST DANGEROUS SPORT, WITH ONE IN EVERY 60 JUMPS ENDING IN DEATH. SURVIVAL IS UNLIKELY ON BASE JUMPS LOWER THAN ABOUT 200 FT (60 M).

Back to base

Why bother with an aircraft, when there's plenty of tall stuff on the ground from which to launch yourself? Base jumping gets its name from the things you can climb to start your plunge—Buildings, Antennas, Spans (bridges), and Earth (cliffs). Base jumpers may be falling for only 10–15 seconds— barely enough time for an ordinary parachute to open. So they jump with special equipment that opens fast and reliably. Despite these precautions, a slight misjudgment can mean a deadly fall.

▲ Spanning a canyon, with a long clear drop below, this road bridge makes an ideal launch point for a base jumper, though he risks arrest if he's caught.

Patterns in the clouds

Formation freefall skydivers aim to link hands and descend in a regular pattern, with each person steering themselves into a prearranged place. Collisions are the biggest danger because they can knock a jumper unconscious, leaving them unable to open their parachute. To combat this, many wear an automatic deployment device that opens their reserve chute at a preset altitude if they don't pull the rip cord.

▶ This 36-way diamond formation drop over Eisenach, Germany, would be perfect... if only those two people at the top had grabbed their buddies' legs!

Below the radar

Special Forces parachutists drop from 25,000 ft (7,600 m). HALO (High-Altitude, Low-Opening) drops offer the least chance of detection, because the soldiers freefall to the lowest safe altitude before opening their parachutes. In HAHO (High-Altitude, High-Opening) drops, their aircraft need not fly over enemy territory. The troops deploy their square, mattress-like chutes quickly, and use them to glide for up to an hour, landing up to 25 mi (40 km) behind enemy lines.

◄ Special Forces jump from such high altitudes that they must breathe bottled oxygen because the air is so thin.

▲ Swiss "Jetman" Yves Rossy has taken wingsuits a huge step further by fitting four engines to a rigid wing. Strapped to his back, it carried him across the English Channel in 2008 at 186 mph (299 km/h).

Soaring on air

Like bats or flying foxes, wingsuit skydivers steer their descent using fabric flaps under their arms and between their legs. These "wings" allow them to fly horizontally, usually zooming 2.5 ft (70 cm) forward for each foot (30 cm) they fall—a glide ratio of 2.5. Wingpacks, made of rigid carbon fiber, can increase the glide ratio to 6. Base jumpers have begun using wingsuits, prolonging their falls from seconds into minutes.

GERMAN BATMAN

Wingpacks are less than 20 years old, but German engineer Otto Lilienthal (1848–1896) pioneered a gliding wing in 1890. He had the bad luck to live in one of the flattest areas of Europe—the North German Plain—so he built an artificial hill from which to fly his batlike craft. Leaping from his *Fliegeberg* (flight-hill) in 1896, Lilienthal rose to 56 ft (17 m), before crashing and breaking his spine. His dying words were "Small sacrifices must be made."

Otto Lilienthal's first gliding trials with his fragile wing took him just a little way off the ground. The more ambitious flights that followed inspired American brothers Orville and Wilbur Wright, who in 1903 built the world's first aircraft.

Playing with FIRE

For once, your parents were right! Playing with fire really is dangerous, so don't try any of these tricks at home. Performers who eat, breathe, and dance with fire have learned their searing skills from experts. They risk painful burns each time they kindle the flames that light up their superhot acts.

▼ Expert fire-eaters put torches right into their mouths, closing their lips to put out the flames.

BREATHING FLAMES

It's not just fearsome legendary beasts that breathe fire. Circus performers spout flames so hot that they need special insurance in case they ignite the audience. To impersonate a dragon, they first take mouthfuls of fuel. Then, taking care to stand with their backs to the wind, they blow across lighted torches, creating spectacular bursts of flame. Burns are the obvious danger, but there are plenty more—swallowing or inhaling fuel can put performers in hospital.

A VERY HOT MEAL

Even the hottest of curries can't rival a feast of fire. Fire-eaters dine on real flames flashing from tapers and torches. How do they do it? There's no trickery involved, and there's no such thing as a "cold flame." It's the fire-eaters' saliva that protects them. By licking their lips and keeping their mouths moist, they create a cooling barrier against the flame's heat.

FANS OF FLAMES

To the Samoans who dance it, *ailao afi* is a modern take on a knife-whirling warrior tradition. To the watching crowd, it's a breathtaking performance of spinning flames and sharp blades. Fire-dancing traditions in Samoa and elsewhere have inspired gymnasts and jugglers to add flaming chains, poles, and hoops to their own acts.

▼ On a darkened stage, flames trace the movements of this Samoan knife fire-dancer.

▶ Firewalking is one of a number of rituals that take place during the Jia Chai festival in Phuket, Thailand.

▲ The pillar of flame from a fire-breather's mouth may burn hotter than 2,000°F (1,100°C).

FIRE-BREATHER ANTONIO RESTIVO BLEW THE WORLD'S BIGGEST FLAME IN JANUARY 2011. AT 26.5 FT (8.05 M), IT WAS AS LONG AS A BUS.

BAREFOOT ORDEAL

In a ceremony that's 3,000 years old, religious people pray for help and protection—then test their faith by walking barefoot on glowing embers! In fact, this "ordeal" is not proof of divine protection. Though the coals may be at 1,700°F (930°C), ashes don't conduct heat well. As long as walkers keep moving, the thick skin on their soles protects their feet. This doesn't mean firewalking is safe—walkers suffer agonizing burns if they trip, or if the coals are ill-prepared.

Death-defying
DIVES

For cliff divers, hitting the water is the end of the thrill, but for breath-hold and ice divers it is just the beginning. However for participants in every form of diving sport, water is a potentially lethal hazard—capable of breaking limbs and sucking air from the lungs.

Daring plunge

What began in 1935 as a tourist-pleasing stunt in Acapulco, Mexico, is now a popular extreme sport. It is the height of the dives that makes cliff-diving extreme. Typically 85 ft (26 m) from the water, the rocky jumping-off points are 2.5 times higher than an Olympic board. Divers plunge at 50–60 mph (85–100 km/h), and to avoid injury they adopt a torpedo-like pose when they enter the water.

MANY FREEDIVERS USE YOGA OR MEDITATION BEFORE A DIVE TO SLOW THEIR METABOLISM AND REDUCE THEIR OXYGEN NEEDS.

▶ In the spectacular drop to the water at Switzerland's narrow Ponte Brolla gorge, Swiss diver Andy Hulliger performed a double back somersault with two twists. This dive—and others—won him fourth place in the 2011 European Cliff Diving Championship.

EVEN FOR PROFESSIONALS, CLIFF DIVING IS RISKY, AND EACH YEAR AMATEUR IMITATORS ARE KILLED OR CRIPPLED.

1 ft Your eardrums flex inward and you feel pressure in your ears

5 ft Water pressure starts to tear the tissue of your eardrums if you lack training

10 ft Pressure on the lungs makes it impossible to suck air down a tube from the surface

20 ft Lung squeeze reverses natural buoyancy, causing you to sink

50 ft Lungs compressed to one quarter of the surface size

Into the deep

How long can you hold your breath? Sixty seconds is pretty good, but the best freedivers can manage eight or nine minutes! Freedivers compete to swim as deep as 870 ft (265 m) without breathing apparatus. In competitions their descents are divided into many categories with different rules. The scariest is No-Limits Apnea, in which the freediver grips a weighted sled to sink like a stone. When they can go no deeper, an air-filled bag brings them to the surface.

▼ The ocean's depths hold no fear for British/Caymanian freediver Tanya Streeter. She holds the women's world record for No-Limits Apnea, with a descent to 525 ft (160 m).

PEARL DIVERS BRING ONE TON OF OYSTERS TO THE WATER'S SURFACE TO FIND JUST THREE OR FOUR PEARLS IN THEIR SHELLS.

Seabed harvest

Breath-hold diving has a long history—3,000 years ago in ancient Greece, salvage divers were given bonuses according to how deep they could swim to retrieve the precious cargoes of sunken galleys. In the centuries that followed, divers held their breath to pluck sponges, pearls, shellfish, and even pirate treasure from the seabed. The invention of scuba (Self-Contained Underwater Breathing Apparatus) in the mid-20th century made these risky diving feats unnecessary.

▼ This breath-hold diver heads for the surface with a net full of black pearl oysters at Fakarava Atoll in French Polynesia. Today's divers don't rely on luck and chance—pearls are farmed here.

BENEATH THE ANTARCTIC

Scientists working in Antarctica dive in temperatures below 32°F (0°C) to study life in the shallow coastal water around the southern continent. Getting into the water isn't easy—they must first use giant augers (drilling tools) to bore holes in the 6-ft- (1.8-m-) thick ice. The water beneath is among the world's clearest, and divers combat its low temperature with dry suits and layered underwear. Getting out can be as hard as getting in—divers must share their ice-holes with fat Weddell seals surfacing to breathe.

▼ Returning to the hole in the ice is vital, so it's marked with a weighted safety line, flags, and flashing lights that divers can see from a great distance away.

Thrill SEEKERS

155

BEASTLY Beasts

This scuba-diving cameraman is taking a grave risk. Tiger sharks are second only to great whites in their record for attacks on humans.

People have lived, worked, and played with wild animals for more than 30,000 years. For most of this time, the beasts got a raw deal, mostly as entertainment for humans. Now that animals in the wild are vanishing fast, we take better care of our savage friends—but interaction with potentially lethal creatures demands extreme caution.

Making friends with Jaws

Long persecuted as killers, sharks are now getting the scientific attention they deserve. They need it—numbers are falling and up to half of all shark species are endangered. Of some 380 shark species, just four are known to attack humans. Scientists study these cautiously. Armored suits protect against a friendly nibble, but when Jaws is big—and hungry—only a cage will do.

Pooch or pack?

British wolf researcher Shaun Ellis has an unconventional approach to studying wolves. To learn about these notorious and misunderstood wild dogs he joined—and led—a wolf pack in Idaho, U.S., learning to live, hunt, eat, and howl just like them. Today he uses his knowledge to help wolves and humans live in harmony in areas where packs' territories are close to people's homes.

At his refuge in Devon, U.K., Shaun Ellis combines research with a TV program to educate the public about wolves and their behavior.

Handlers carry "weapons," but do not hurt the dogs they train.

He's only playing!

In the cruel and illegal "sport" of dogfighting, owners *try* to make their dogs aggressive, but not all attack dogs are savage. The police and the military use dogs for law enforcement and security. Living suspects are more useful than dead ones, so handlers train their canine colleagues to chase and hold onto fleeing villains, slowing them down until an officer arrives. It shouldn't hurt, but trainers wear padded clothes, just in case.

Spots or stripes?

Studying large predators in the wild is a risky business, and scientists have to take care to avoid being confused with their subjects' natural prey. They use box traps and tranquilizer darts to make animals safe to handle, then often tag them for radio tracking. Even a tagged animal can be a danger—the tracking receiver shows only direction, not distance, and isn't accurate when the tagged animal is very nearby.

▲ Scientists in Colorado, U.S., release a captured lynx into its natural environment after fitting it with a radio collar to track its movements.

KAZAKHSTAN FALCONERS RAISE BIRDS FROM CHICKS, RISKING THEIR LIVES TO TAKE THEM FROM NESTS ON REMOTE CRAGS.

▼ Thick gloves protect a Kazakhstani falconer's outstretched arms from the sharp talons of his beloved eagle.

Swooping hunters

In medieval Europe, falconry was considered the noblest of the hunting arts. The more noble the nobleman, the bigger the bird that perched on his gloved fist. This must make today's Kazakhstan hunters the royalty of falconers, for they hunt with the world's biggest raptors—golden eagles. These powerful birds weigh as much as a small turkey, and have a 7 ft (2 m) wingspan.

SERIOUS
Summits

Watch a skilled climber scale a rock wall, and you'll realize why this demanding sport has been nicknamed the "vertical dance." The elegant, graceful movements of top mountaineers are not just for show. They conserve energy, keep the climbers balanced, and—most importantly—protect them from potentially fatal falls.

Defying gravity

Clinging by your fingertips from vertical rock may look risky, but expert climbers fix their safety ropes to anchors (metal devices wedged in the rock) at regular intervals. Although this technique (known as "lead climbing") reduces risk, a leader who slips will fall the distance to their latest starting point, plus the slack of the rope. However, even on popular and dizzyingly high rock faces, fatal accidents are rare, because experienced climbers tutor novices in safety and caution.

IN THE "DEATH ZONE," ABOVE 26,000 FT (8,000 M), THE AIR IS SO THIN THAT NO CLIMBER CAN SURVIVE FOR LONG.

◄ To get up ice walls like this cave in Iceland's Langjökull glacier, climbers use hollow ice screws. They turn them securely into the ice, then fix safety ropes through rings at the ends.

◄ "Soloing" (climbing without the protection of a safety rope) on a route such as El Cap in Yosemite Park, U.S., is highly dangerous—a single error could lead to a fatal fall.

Super-slippery slope

Ice is as slippy as rock is grippy, so winter climbing requires different techniques. Even on quite gentle slopes an ice climber needs crampons—sharp spikes fixed to boot soles. To get up really steep slopes such as frozen waterfalls, climbers swing special pointed axes into the ice, looping safety ropes through protection (anchors) screwed into the frozen surface.

"Because it's there"

The world's great peaks are often in remote locations. Reaching them means days of walking, carrying everything you need for the whole trip. The atmosphere gets thinner the higher you go, forcing climbers to gulp oxygen from gas bottles. So why climb a high mountain? English climber George Mallory famously answered "because it's there" before climbing the world's highest peak, Everest.

▶ Mallory (shown here in the Alps) probably reached Everest's summit in 1924, but he and his partner Sandy Irvine died while descending the mountain.

High, light, and fast

Italian climber Reinhold Messner leads the world in Alpinism—the art of climbing fast, high, and with few supplies and equipment. In May 1978, he and fellow climber Peter Habeler climbed Everest without bottled oxygen, a feat previously considered impossible. Two years later Messner did it again—alone!

▲ The greatest climber of all time, Messner was the first to ascend all the world's peaks higher than 26,000 ft (8,000 m). Here he points to Everest soon after his lone ascent.

Pioneer of the peaks

The thin air of high mountains causes altitude sickness. Those affected suffer blinding headaches, exhaustion, dizziness, and confusion. German explorer and mountaineer Alexander von Humboldt was the first to describe it, after climbing Ecuador's Chimborazo volcano in 1802. This wasn't the only hardship he suffered in South America. He dodged vampire bats, cannibals, alligators, and a club-waving madman!

▶ German explorer and naturalist Alexander von Humboldt (1769–1859) gave his name to a dozen places and almost as many natural features.

Symptoms of altitude sickness

1. Headaches (may even appear at the altitude of a ski resort).

2. Climbing higher causes dizziness, tiredness, and breathlessness.

3. Hands and feet swell and the nose bleeds.

4. In severe altitude sickness, sufferers get a dry cough they can't shake. Headaches worsen and nausea begins.

5. Extreme altitude eventually kills climbers—fluid collects in their tissues, causing the brain to swell.

High-flying THRILLS

S oaring, spinning, leaping, and balancing high above the ring, circus acrobats risk deadly falls twice daily to entertain big-top audiences. Safety nets or harnesses can break a fall, but do not completely remove the danger, and the most daring aerial artists perform without protection at alarming heights.

▶ These two young performers from the Chinese State Circus are using parasols to help keep their balance on the high wire.

▶ Gymnasts performing on silks use thick fabric, which is at least 5 ft (1.5 m) wide.

Ropes and silks

Though more gymnastic than acrobatic, free-hanging rope or ribbon acts expose the performer to dangerous, unbroken falls. Mastery of these acts involves learning to climb from the ground, gripping and balancing on the rope or ribbon without using the hands, and—most demanding of all—releasing it to drop suddenly down in a controlled spin. Performers use rosin (pine resin) to increase their grip.

HIGH HISTORY

Legendary French acrobat Charles Blondin set a standard for rope-walking that has never been equaled. His most famous feat, performed in 1859, was to cross America's Niagara Falls on a 1,100-ft- (335-m-) long rope. Simply walking across was too simple for Blondin—he also did it blindfolded, pushing a wheelbarrow, on stilts, and carrying his manager on his back. He even stopped in the middle to cook and eat an omelet.

▼ Stretched tight 160 ft (almost 50 m) above the churning waterfall, Blondin's rope was the width of a person's forearm.

Big-top balance

Invented in China, rope-walking is the most ancient form of altitude acrobatics. It was popular in ancient Rome—2nd-century emperor Marcus Aurelius passed a law that forced rope-walkers to use a safety net. Today, a steel wire has replaced the traditional rope, and stabilizer cables stop it swaying on long spans. Walkers also use a bar to help them balance and to walk in winds that would otherwise be dangerous.

Playing catch

The most gripping aerial act is the flying trapeze, in which performers hurl and catch each other high above the crowd. The flyer must be nimble and light, the catcher must be strong, and timing is vital for all involved. Almost all trapeze artists perform above nets, but an awkward fall to the net may cause serious injury.

> TRAPEZE ARTISTS HURTLE THROUGH THE AIR AT SPEEDS OF MORE THAN 60 MPH (100 KM/H).

▼ Cable-car lines are ready-made for high-wire acts. In 2009 Swiss wire-walker Freddy Nock climbed one to the top of the Zugspitze, Germany's highest peak.

Taking it outside

Outdoor high-wire acts require special preparation. The team rigging the wire must be sure that the anchor points at each end are strong enough to take the enormous tension in the wire without breaking. Wires have additional diagonal cables to stop them swaying in the wind. Even with these precautions performers are at considerable risk—and must even check the weather forecast for lightning warnings.

Thrill SEEKERS

BLADES and POINTS

In a crowded street, a half-naked performer chops a cabbage in two with a long blade, then tips back his head and slowly eats... the sword! There's no trick involved—sword swallowing and other sharp-edged acts such as walking on glass are genuine feats of daring, and highly dangerous for the untrained.

Dancing with scissors

In remote mountain villages of Peru, the *danza de la tijeras* (scissors dance) is half competition, half folk ritual. The traditional dancers snip at the air around them with iron rods like scissors in contests that may continue all day. In their most extreme form, the dances become flesh-tearing ordeals in which men demonstrate how much pain they can endure. In 2010 UNESCO recognized the dance as a unique part of Peru's cultural heritage.

▶ The dances may celebrate the pagan gods worshipped before the Spanish conquest of Peru in the 16th century.

Hunger pangs

Swallowing swords was once thought to be a trick, but the invention of X-ray photography showed that the blade really does go all the way down. Students of the art start by tickling their throats with small pieces of wire. This teaches them to overcome the gag reflex—the automatic tightening of the throat that normally stops us choking on food. To swallow a blade safely, they must straighten their necks so that the mouth, throat, and stomach lie in a straight line.

▶ An X-ray image of Australian stunt performer Chayne Hultgren, AKA The Space Cowboy, clearly shows the long blade he has swallowed. The Space Cowboy also swallows table legs, saws, neon lights, and hedge clippers.

Light lunch

Expert glass-chewers take care to crunch a lightbulb into very fine pieces, as swallowing bigger chunks can damage the throat and gut. Performers who specialize in eating strange objects don't stop at glass. Frenchman "Monsieur Mangetout" has eaten a bicycle, a shopping trolley, and a light aircraft.

▲ Chinese stuntman Zhang Yujian takes just 40 seconds to crunch his way through a 60-watt bulb.

SOLE SURVIVOR

Leathery feet are an advantage when it comes to walking on broken glass, but careful preparation is just as important. Performers use clean broken bottles, and move the tough, angular bases and corners to the edge of the track. A deep bed of glass ensures that it can shift underfoot, reducing the risk of sharp edges pointing upward. "Feeling the way" with the feet enables glass-walkers to shift their weight away from the sharpest pieces.

▼ At a performance in Paris, Cirque de Pekin stars put a new twist on the bed-of-nails stunt.

Sleep well

Once the speciality of Indian fakirs (Muslim holy men), lying on a bed of nails actually requires no religious faith. Though the nails are sharp, they are very closely spaced, so there is not enough pressure on a single nail to pierce the skin. However, the stunt is safe only if the performer's weight is evenly spread on the "bed." The difficult part is getting on and off—sudden movements can cause prickly problems.

Going for the RECORD

SPEEDY
DOWNHILL CYCLE
Stöckl set a new world record for mountain bikes in La Parva, Chile, when he hit a speed of 130.7 mph (210.4 km/h) in 2007.

Want to pilot the fastest human-powered vehicle on land, water, or air? Then start pedaling! Spinning the cranks is the most efficient way to turn muscle power into movement, whether you're on the road, in an aircraft, or in a submarine. So between record attempts, you'll find speed heroes out training on their bikes.

Where are the brakes?

Mountain bikers relish a steep hill, but few dare to tackle slopes as steep and treacherous as those Eric Barone chooses. This French cyclist holds the world record for speedy descents on wheels. He hurtles down volcanoes and snowy peaks as fast as an express train. Specially customized bikes, including enhanced brakes, give a competitive edge

▶ Austrian Markus Stöckl holds world records for descents on unmodified mountain bikes.

THE INCREDIBLE SPEED AND BONE-JOLTING SHOCKS OF EXTREME DOWNHILL RIDES CAN LITERALLY SHAKE A BIKE TO PIECES.

Laid-back pedaler

It's a bike, but not as we know it! Ordinary, or "diamond frame," bicycles are just too slow to break records on level courses, as their high saddle positions create air resistance that slows them down. Instead, the world's fastest bikers lie back to pedal, powering their "recumbent" bikes at more than 80 mph (130 km/h) A streamlined fairing (covering) makes the bike look—and perform—like a bullet.

▼ At 83 mph (133.5 km/h), Sam Whittingham is the fastest self-propelled person on the planet.

FASTEST
LEVEL LAND SPEED
Canadian Sam Whittingham took the world 200 m speed record for a human-powered vehicle in September 2009.

Up, up, and away

Compared to record-breaking bikes, human-powered aircraft move at a very leisurely pace. What's extraordinary is that they fly at all—they look as fragile as cobwebs. Builders shave every ounce of weight from the airframe so that the pilot's vigorous pedaling can lift himself and the 100-ft- (30-m-) wide plane just a few feet into the air. Flight alone isn't enough—to win prizes, the plane must navigate a figure-of-eight course.

FIRST
HUMAN-POWERED PLANE
Gossamer Condor completed a one-mile (1.6-km) course using nothing but pedal power.

◄ Pilot Bryan Allen is a cyclist and hang-glider enthusiast, so he was the perfect choice to pedal aircraft *Gossamer Condor* on a prize-winning flight in August 1977.

COOLEST
HUMAN-POWERED SUB
The *FAU-Boat* narrowly scooped the speed prize in 1993, beating its competitor by just 15 seconds.

Blowing bubbles

Since 1989, submarine enthusiasts have been competing to be the fastest human under water at races organized in the U.S. by the Foundation for Underwater Research and Education (FURE). Dozens of shark-shaped subs take part, each with one or two crew members turning the pedal-powered propellers. The subs are flooded with water on the 330-ft (100-m) course, and the crew breathe using SCUBA masks. The winning subs speed along at 9 mph (14 km/h) or faster.

◄ The colorful *FAU-Boat*, an entry from the Florida Atlantic University, speeds to victory at the 3rd International Submarine Races.

FASTEST
OLYMPIC SPORT
American Tony Benshoof holds the world luge speed record of 86.93 mph (139.9 km/h).

▼ Luge athletes have to cope with steep turns in the track as well as blistering speed.

Slippery slope

The fastest of all Olympic athletes don't need pedals—they rely on gravity to speed them down a hillside track glazed with ice. Luge racers lie on their backs on a sled no bigger than a tea tray. They expertly flex the sled to guide its runners. The sport of luge began in the late 19th century in the frozen streets and lanes of Swiss town St. Moritz. Today competitive races are all held on purpose-built ice tracks.

DYING
to Win

Which is more risky, jogging or skydiving? The answer may surprise you: traffic and other hazards mean you're more likely to die pounding the pavement than leaping out of a plane. Even with strict rules to promote safety, top athletes have to be super-skilled—and have a bit of luck—to stay injury-free.

Brain bangers

Strict rules, fist and face padding, and medical help make boxing safer than the bare-knuckle fistfights of the sport's origins. However, the boxing ring is still a bloody, wild place. The knockout blow to the head that wins a bout can cause permanent brain injury. Damage shows up on brain scans of four out of every five professional boxers.

▲ In this 2007 match Mexican Oscar Larios (right) took a pounding from his rival that knocked him to the floor, and lost him the contest.

▼ In matches like this international game between France and Japan, scrums are safer because the teams are equally strong. Mismatched teams are more at risk.

No protection required

Rugby players don't wear the heavy padding that protects those in NFL (National Football League) games, so you would expect them to suffer more blood, bruises, and broken bones. In fact, lack of protection makes rugby less aggressive. Scrums (when teams lock arms and heads to push and gain ground) are the most dangerous part of the game, especially when players' strength and size are unequal. If the scrum collapses, front-row players risk serious injury.

Gridiron hazards

Crrrunch! The bone-splitting sound of a tackle tells you all you need to know. The strength and aggression that's needed to succeed in American football makes it a risky game. Thanks to helmets and padding fatalities are low, but injuries remain common. Head injuries, in particular, often go unnoticed, and professional NFL players may suffer hidden brain damage that handicaps them long after their careers are over.

▶ Quentin Jammer makes a flying tackle in this match between the New England Patriots and the San Diego Chargers.

▶ Jockey W. J. Lee didn't stay long in the saddle in this 2011 race. Professional horse racing is one of the most risky sports and jockeys suffer three injuries in an average year.

Giddy up!

The dangers of being a champion jockey are obvious—high jumps and high speed can make falls fatal. But ordinary horse-riding is dangerous, too, and 120 Americans die each year in riding accidents. Horses are unpredictable and it's a long way from the saddle to the ground. So should horse-riding be banned as a dangerous sport? No! You are seven times more likely to die by choking on your food!

Jungle grotto

Some of the world's most fantastic cave systems are doubly hidden. Not only are their vast tunnel networks out of sight beneath the ground, but the entrances are buried deep in remote forests. Reaching these inaccessible caves may involve long treks through dripping jungle, carrying supplies and heavy kit. Hang Son Doong, in central Vietnam, was used as a shelter during the country's 1960s war, but locals soon forgot the cave when bombing stopped. It took cavers three expeditions just to find the entrance.

▲ Rediscovered in 2009, Son Doong (Mountain River) Cave encloses a fast-flowing river, which creates an eerie whistle at the entrance. At 660 ft (200 m) in height, the biggest chamber is the largest in any cave in the world.

Into the EARTH

They are cramped, wet, cold, dangerous, and totally dark—so exactly what is the attraction of caves? The thrill of venturing into truly unexplored territory is one reason why these intrepid subterranean sportsmen spend their lives—and savings—exploring the world's deepest natural tunnels.

Muddy squeeze

Protective clothing such as boots, overalls, and a helmet are essentials for moving through low, muddy, narrow passages. One helmet light is not enough, and many cavers carry a third. Even with this basic equipment, you should never start exploring caves without the help of someone who's been underground before, and never go down alone.

▲ The Krubera cave in Georgia's Caucasus Mountains burrows deeper into the earth than any other. The deepest point explorers have reached is 7,200 ft (2,200 m) below the entrance.

Rock-climbing upside down

Deep cave systems include long vertical drops that are difficult or impossible to descend or ascend using ordinary rock-climbing techniques. To tackle these obstacles, cavers must use either fold-up ladders or ascenders—devices that slide up a fixed rope, but clamp tight when pulled down. With loops of rope hung from a pair of ascenders, cavers can laboriously pull themselves up from great depths.

▲ Jagged stalactites (hanging points of rock) make the roofs of cave passages an uncomfortable obstacle. In this Thailand tunnel the caver pushes an oxygen tank ahead of her.

Deep, dark water

Flooded tunnels make a dangerous cave potentially deadly. Cavers use SCUBA equipment, but—unlike ocean divers—they cannot surface if the air runs out. There are other risks—the water can be very cold and fast-flowing, and mud can suddenly reduce visibility to zero in a "silt out." Training and specialized equipment help to reduce the risk, and cave divers tackle silt outs by letting out a guideline as they move forward. Even if mud blinds them, they can follow the line back to safety.

▲ Top cave divers endure some of the toughest environments on the planet, exploring icy cold and uncharted waters.

All at SEA

ROUTES

━━━ First solo circumnavigation (Joshua Slocum)

━━━ First nonstop circumnavigation (Chay Blyth)

━━━ Swimming the Channel (David Walliams)

━━━ Rowing the Pacific (Roz Savage)

━━━ Vendée Globe race

Sailors and swimmers who cross the world's deep waters risk drowning, exhaustion, and loneliness. So why do they do it? For many of them, it's the challenge of beating a record that drives them on. For others, it's a way of testing themselves, or achieving a long-held personal ambition.

NORTH ATLANTIC OCEAN

Boston, U.S.
Joshua Slocum start/finish

Southampton, U.K.
Chay Blyth start/finish

San Francisco, U.S.
Roz Savage Pacific crossing start

PACIFIC OCEAN

Roz Savage

Hawaii

Les Sables-d'Olonne, France
Vendée Globe race start/finish

Who started it all?

Solo voyages around the world began at the end of the 19th century with the adventures of Canadian-American seaman and boat-builder Joshua Slocum (1844–1909). In April 1895 he set sail in the *Spray*, a 37-ft (11-m) oyster boat that he had rebuilt himself. Using centuries-old navigation methods he took three years to complete the voyage.

Joshua Slocum

▶ Slocum described the huge wave that engulfed his tiny boat off South America: "She shook in every timber and reeled under the weight of the sea."

SOUTH ATLANTIC OCEAN

Chay Blyth

Round the world, the hard way

Circumnavigation (circling the world) in a sailing boat is a dangerous, difficult task. Doing it alone, and without docking at a port, is harder still. And heading westward piles on even more risk, for the boat must sail into the wind for most of the route. The first successful attempt came in 1971, when Scottish sailor Chay Blyth completed the trip in 292 days.

SOUTHERN OCEAN

Vendée Globe race

▶ Sailing in his yacht *Adrien*, French sailor Jean Luc van den Heede clipped a month from the world single-handed record for the westward round-the-world route in 2004. It took him 122 days.

Open water

To understand the challenge facing an open-water swimmer, measure their epic crossings in pool lengths. Swimming the Cook Strait between New Zealand's two islands is equivalent to 440 Olympic pool lengths. The English Channel is 675. But distance—and the tiredness and cramp it brings—is just half of the difficulty. Swimmers also brave bone-numbing cold, debris in the water, shipping, jellyfish, and sharks.

◄ British comedian David Walliams didn't break any records when he swam the English Channel in 2006, but he raised £1m ($1.5m) for charity.

Rowing the widest ocean

Most people who have rowed across an ocean haven't done so by choice—shipwreck forced them to pull on the oars or perish. Two Norwegians rowed across the Atlantic by choice in 1896, and transatlantic races began in 1997. At 7,000 mi (12,000 km) across, the Pacific is four times wider than the Atlantic. John Fairfax and Sylvia Cook were the first to cross it, from San Francisco, U.S., to Hayman Island, Australia, in 1971. They were rowing for 361 days.

▼ Roz Savage became the first woman to row across the Pacific single handed in 2010. She split her voyage into three legs, arriving in Waikiki, Hawaii (below), at the end of the first stage, one million oar strokes after leaving the Californian coast.

Roz Savage → *Tarawa*

Papua New Guinea Roz Savage Pacific crossing finish

PACIFIC OCEAN

Joshua Slocum

INDIAN OCEAN

Chay Blyth

Vendée Globe race

Braving icebergs

Today, single-handed sailing around the world has become a sport. In the Vendée Globe race, solo yachtsmen and women sail from France to the Southern Ocean, race clockwise around Antarctica, and return home—all without assistance. It's a grueling, hazardous competition. High winds, monstrous waves, and sea ice force mariners to be constantly alert. None of the skippers dare sleep—instead they take short naps five or six times a day.

▼ The VM Matériaux, sailed by Patrice Carpentier, crosses the starting line to begin the Vendée Globe race. A broken boom later put him out of the race.

RISKS on Screen

Some moviegoers are becoming indifferent to special effects that they know are computer-generated, so many directors are turning back to old-fashioned stunts. Now when you see a star get shot, burned, blown up, or hurled off a building, there's a good chance that a stunt double risked their life to make the scene convincing.

Up in flames

Performing in burning clothes is one of the most dangerous of all stunts. Doubles wear several layers of fireproof clothing over their skin, then don a flesh-colored mask and gloves. Gel fuel on the costume makes the flames. Flames use up oxygen, so the double uses a mouthpiece to breathe air from a hidden cylinder. Because of the danger of the stunt, shots last only seconds before crews with fire extinguishers put out the flames.

▼ Wreathed in flames, a stuntman wrestles to remove his helmet in the stunt show *Moteurs*.

Boom BOOM!

Exploding vehicles are too dangerous for doubles, so gasoline-filled mannequins take their place at the wheel. However, doubles may drive cars lifted by explosions. Pyrotechnics experts rig a section of a telegraph pole behind the car, with an explosive charge above it. Detonating the charge fires the pole into the ground, flipping the car.

▲ Thirteen stunt doubles helped add live action realism to the 2005 German action movie *Der Clown*.

WAS THAT ME?

For a major star's stunt double, a likeness of face and physique is an advantage, but it's not absolutely essential. Makeup hides differences and directors can line up shots so that the double's face appears on screen only briefly, or not at all. Skilful cutting-in of close-ups of the real star seamlessly conceals the substitution.

◀ American actor Tom Cruise would have risked serious injury in this shot of a motorcycle wheelie, so a stunt double took his place.

Happy landings

In the early days of movie stunts, doubles who fell or jumped from heights landed on carefully stacked piles of cardboard boxes. Today, airbags break their fall. For longer drops a double will hang from a steel cable wrapped round the drum of a fan descender. As the cable unwinds, fan vanes fixed to the drum slow its spin, so that the double falls at a safe, but still convincing, speed.

◀ When Johnny Depp's double jumped from a window in *The Tourist* (2010), a canvas awning and a heap of vegetables broke his fall.

ROUGHLY FOUR STUNTMEN DIE ON FILM SETS EACH YEAR. BUT MANY MORE ARE INJURED.

▶ A career as a stuntman doesn't have to be painful and short. Greg Brazzell, who is driving this car, has made 90 films.

Hitting the asphalt

Car chases and stunts start with careful preparation of the vehicles. Mechanics strengthen the car's structure and enhance the springs and shock absorbers. They may also enhance the engine's performance. Then it's down to the driving skills of stunt doubles to put the cars where the director wants them. Stars rarely drive, even if they are experts behind the wheel, as an accident would put the whole movie at risk.

173

SNOW Business

For skiers who find even the most demanding routes too tame, mountaintops still have plenty to offer, though the risks are as high as the summits. Beyond the reach of the lifts, slopes wind down through obstacles such as trees and vertical cliffs, and simple mistakes can trigger a deadly fall—or an avalanche.

Board or bored?

Not long ago, skiers scorned snowboarders as inferior intruders to the slopes. Today boarding is mainstream, with resorts offering rails, half-pipes, and jumps for enthusiasts. To the hardcore boarder this "taming" of their sport is unwelcome. The most skilled are following steep skiers to higher and more vertical runs. Though some compete in races, much of the pleasure of extreme snowboarding comes from the isolation and emptiness of remote slopes.

▶ Resorts make learning snowboarding (relatively) painless. At this New Zealand ski field, novices practice flying moves with an air-mattress to protect their limbs.

Getting airborne

Leaving the snow far below is part of the thrill in all forms of extreme skiing, but in ski jumping and ski flying nothing else matters. Skiers plummet down purpose-built hills, reaching more than 60 mph (100 km/h) before taking off into the air, so landing is a critical skill. Ski flying places more emphasis on how you float through the air, though distance still matters—the world record-holder, Norwegian Johan Evensen, has soared 800 ft (250 m).

▼ To a holiday skier, the view from a ski jumping hill is terrifying. Here Johan Evensen of Norway gazes down the 400-ft (120-m) drop at Oslo's Holmenkollen Ski Arena.

Chopper me up

Lifts and graded, groomed slopes make ski holidays popular and convenient, but they also create crowds. Skiers who crave empty, unspoiled surroundings now use helicopters to escape the resorts and ski ever-higher terrain. The lower temperatures at higher altitudes ensure that the snow is deeper, and for those who can afford it, it's the ultimate skiing experience.

▶ Launching yourself into deep, white powder as the chopper powers away above your head is the ultimate ski thrill.

◀ On familiar mountains, steep skiers know every crag, and can confidently jump from cliffs like this one in Banff National Park, Canada. For visitors, though, a mountain guide is essential.

WHITE DEATH

Off-piste skiers risk dislodging deep snow on higher slopes, sending it down the mountain as an avalanche. Avalanches can bury skiers, trapping them so tightly that they cannot move or breathe. Finding avalanche victims is a slow process—ten people take an hour to search an area the size of a tennis court. Few survive beneath the snow for even half this time. To improve their chances of being found, off-piste skiers carry emergency radio beacons.

AN AVALANCHE CASCADING DOWN A MOUNTAINSIDE HAS MORE THAN HALF THE POWER OF THE ENGINES THAT LIFTED THE SPACE SHUTTLE INTO ORBIT.

Beyond black diamonds

The steepest regular trails, marked by twin black diamonds, have slopes of 45–50°. They are vertiginous enough to strike terror into the heart of even very experienced skiers. To extreme skiers, these are the warm-up slopes. The real fun begins when the slope is 60° and over. The routes they choose are all off piste—not pressed into tracks. These make extremely long, fast descents possible, with many chances to go big—perform jumps with controlled landings.

WINGS of Victory

Air racers and aerobatic teams trace their roots back over a century to the days of wire-and-canvas planes. Today's pilots fly high-performance jet and prop aircraft. Their nail-biting displays of daring, speed, and precision take them low over ground and water, or in tight-formation passes above the watching crowds.

Barnstormers and wing-walkers

When World War I ended in 1918, the U.S. government sold off hundreds of surplus aircraft. Curtis JN-4s, or "Jennies," were slower and less powerful than a small modern car. Former air force pilots began using them for barnstorming—air tricks at farming fairs. The planes' slow speed enabled pilots to perform stunts such as jumping from car to plane. Modern stunt pilots repeat Jenny performances such as wing-walking.

▲ Stunt flyers really did stand on wings for pictures, but the rackets were a pose—the slipstream would have blown the ball away.

Wingtip to wingtip

Trailing colored smoke and accompanied by earsplitting roars, an aerobatic team soars so low overhead that the airshow crowds instinctively duck. These spectacular displays are performed only by military teams because of the prohibitive cost of the jet trainers they use. Pilots are the air force elite, and must fly at least 1,500 hours before they can even apply to join the team. Only one applicant in ten is chosen. Accidents are rare, but all pilots wear parachutes for both displays and training.

1920'S FLYING TEAM 13 BLACK CATS HAD A PRICE LIST FOR STUNTS. MOST COSTLY WAS $1,500 (£960) FOR BLOWING UP THE PLANE IN MIDAIR.

▲ The Royal Air Force Red Arrows aerobatic team fly their Hawk trainers in tight formation at displays worldwide. Their support crew outnumber the nine pilots ten-to-one.

Over 200 miles per hour

International Air Races
St·Louis ~
October 1·2·3

AERONAUTICAL
EXHIBITION
AERO CONGRESS
AIR INSTITUTE
VEILED PROPHET

▲ Speeds on the graphic posters for the original air races seem quaint today, but in the 1920s, 200 mph (320 km/h) was mind-numbingly fast.

Once around the block

Racing aircraft round a circuit of pylons (tall wooden towers) began in the 1920s. At first a simple task, the difficulty and danger grew as aircraft became faster and more powerful. In modern contests, such as the Reno Air Races, pilots lap the circuits at a blistering 500 mph (800 km/h). Because of the high speeds and low altitudes at which the aircraft fly, crashes are often deadly.

▶ American pilot Michael Goulian, who is flying this Zivko Edge 540 race plane, comes from a family of pilots. He learned to fly a plane before he could drive.

▼ Fighter aircraft like these F-16s can push pilots' bodies to the limit. As well as using g-suits, pilots tense their muscles to stay conscious.

Pulling gs

Making a tight turn forces jet pilots down into their seats, as if the force of gravity had increased, multiplying their weight. The force is measured in gs: 2 g is a doubling of gravity. High g-forces make a pilot's blood flow away from the brain, starving it of vital oxygen. At 5 or 6 g, pilots can lose consciousness. To prevent this, they wear tight g-suits with inflatable panels in the legs. In tight turns these automatically fill with air, squeezing blood back up to the brain.

Ultimate
STREET SPORTS

In organized—and televised—contests for street sports, judges give out points and prizes for skill, agility, and speed. But on the street, it's the hard, unyielding materials of the sidewalk that are the real judges. There are no second chances with concrete and tarmac, and any seasoned urban athlete has the scars to prove it.

▶ Parkour traceurs (participants) emphasize speed and efficiency, while free-runners are bigger on stunts and tricks.

LEAP OF FAITH

You can gauge how fashionable a sport has become by the number of appearances it makes in movies and commercials. By this measure, you can't get much cooler than parkour and free-running. They demand similar skills of nimbleness, fitness, judgment, and individual style. Using vaults, flips, spins, and rolls, athletes aim to move through a city with the grace of dancers.

PARKOUR'S FOUNDERS SAY THEY THINK OF THEIR SPORT AS AN ARTFORM, AND DESCRIBE THE URBAN ENVIRONMENT AS "A PLAYGROUND."

Not for safety freaks

Urban downhill mountain biking swaps steep, muddy slopes for concrete stairs. To withstand the pace, bikes have lightweight but strengthened frames with front suspension only. Competitions, such as the hair-raising Valparaiso Cerro Abajo in Chile, are run over specially constructed courses with plywood obstacles. Amateur riders can get the practice they need in sloping streets and abandoned buildings of practically any city.

◀ At the 9th Valparaiso urban downhill race in 2011 in Chile, the watching crowd get dangerously close to the speeding competitors.

Spiderman for real

Rock faces are thin on the ground in cities, but skyscrapers can be the next best thing for serious climbers. Architectural features provide hand and foot holds and anchor points—to scale New York's World Trade Center in 1977, climber George Willig fixed clamps to the window-cleaning rails. Urban climbing is sometimes called buildering—a pun on practice climbs over boulders.

▲ Alain Robert first climbed this 32-story block in Frankfurt, Germany, in 1995. Here, 13 years on, he repeats the feat with a safety rope—and the permission of the owner, Dresdner Bank.

◀ Though it peaked in the 80s, skateboarding still has a hard core of active fans.

BIG AIR

When most people look at a city street they see curbs, walkways, rails, and benches. But through the eyes of a skateboarder the same street is a series of athletic challenges and a wealth of opportunities for stunts and tricks. Extreme streetboarding pushes this urban sport to the limit, with experts performing maneuvers that seem to defy gravity. Most escape serious injury—it's the beginners who end up kissing the concrete.

Tear up the tarmac

Street luge takes its name from the sledge on which winter sports athletes plunge down a frozen track. In street luge, though, wheels and tarmac take the place of runners and ice. Gravity causes the adapted skateboards and their riders to hurtle downhill at up to 70 mph (110 km/h)— fast enough that friction can literally melt wheels.

▲ Street luge riders wear motorcycle leathers to avoid road rash.

Cheating DEATH!

To free themselves from ropes, straitjackets, chains, and prison cells, escapologists need to be fit, nimble, and skilled at picking locks and handcuffs. The traditions of their craft date back to the 18th century, but modern escapologists have added sensational twists to bring them into their acts to bring them into the age of TV and the web.

NO LOCK COULD HOLD HIM!

Harry Houdini was so famous that his name has become a word—"a Houdini" is any ingenious escape. The man behind the legend was a Hungarian-American who boasted no lock could hold him. In a career lasting 35 years he escaped from chains, boxes, mailbags, graves, and water-filled tanks, as well ropes and handcuffs. Houdini also claimed he could take a blow from anyone's fist, but in 1926 a student punched him before he could prepare himself and he died from an infection the next day.

EUROPE'S ECLIPSING SENSATION
HOUDINI
THE WORLD'S HANDCUFF KING & PRISON BREAKER

"NOTHING ON EARTH CAN HOLD HOUDINI A PRISONER"

BIG FREEZE!

DEEP DANGER!

180

DO OR DIE

Modern escapologists have to do much more than just escape—they need to be all-round entertainers. Houdini's audiences were content to watch a curtain for half an hour while he escaped behind it, but today this would seem ridiculous. Escape artists now perform in full view, and usually also add another attraction to their act, such as magic. Some of them, such as Thomas Solomon, deliberately avoid Houdini's escapes, while others perform them with new, dangerous features. They don't reveal their secrets, though Solomon admits to using the magician's old trick of misdirection—he distracts his audience at a crucial moment, so that they overlook the move that frees him.

DIY ESCAPES

Escapes from handcuffs and ropes are the easiest to perform. Handcuffs are kept tight around the wrists by a simple click-latch. To open the latch, escapologists just slide in a shim—a sliver of metal small enough to hide under the tongue. Knots are almost as easy—during the knotting, deep breaths and muscle tension expand the escapologist's body. After relaxing and breathing out, they can wriggle free.

DAVID MERLINI

Equipped with hammers and blowtorches, David Merlini's crew free him from the block of ice in which he has been frozen for half an hour. This 2001 stunt is among the most spectacular that the Hungarian escapologist has performed.

DAVID BLAINE

Endlessly inventive, American David Blaine is one of the world's most high-profile escape artists. In 2006, he was chained to a gyroscope near Times Square in New York, U.S. He freed himself after two days and nights of spinning.

CONSENTINO

Australian escape artist "Consentino" is a self-taught illusionist. His 2010 escape from chains and handcuffs in Melbourne's shark-infested aquarium was a tribute to Houdini's plunge from the city's Queens Bridge a century earlier.

DEAN GUNNARSON

Harry Houdini invented the hanging straitjacket escape, but modern escapologists like Dean Gunnarson take it to another level. In this performance in Melbourne, Australia, the rope burns as he struggles to free himself from chains high above the ground.

Survival
OF THE FITTEST

The world is running out of truly unexplored places—an airliner can fly to anywhere on the globe within 24 hours. But this doesn't spell the end of adventure, or risk. Ice, rock, ocean, and jungle wilderness still beckon the brave, and the stories of their ordeals and narrow escapes inspire those of us who dare not follow them.

MOUNTAIN ODYSSEY

Your buddy hangs from a safety rope. If you cut it, you might live. If you don't, you'll both die. What would you do?

The climb, and the agonizing decision that Simon Yates took, were turned into the gripping 1983 movie *Touching the Void*.

This was the awful choice facing Simon Yates in the Peruvian Andes in 1985. He and Joe Simpson were climbing the 20,813-ft (6,344-m) Siula Grande. They reached the summit, and were on the descent when Joe slipped and broke his leg.

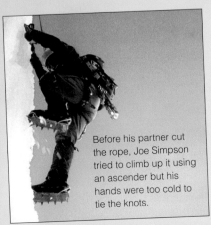

Before his partner cut the rope, Joe Simpson tried to climb up it using an ascender but his hands were too cold to tie the knots.

Simon began lowering Joe on two knotted ropes, but the injured climber went over a cliff. The two could not see or hear each other. There was no way Simon could save his buddy, so he made the dreadful decision to cut the rope. Simon spent another night on the mountain before descending to their base camp. Feeling fearful and guilty, he looked for his climbing partner but there was no sign of him. Simon decided that Joe must have died in the fall. But Joe had survived. When the rope went slack he plunged into a crevasse, dug a snow cave, and fell asleep. When he awoke, he began an epic three-day journey, without food and with very little water. Nursing his injured leg, he crawled and hopped the 5 mi (8 km) back to base camp, arriving just hours before Simon planned to pack up the camp and leave.

Struck down in the Pacific

For a couple of seasoned sailors like Richard Sharp and his fiancée Tami Oldham, it sounded like the dream job: a four-week cruise from Tahiti, delivering a luxury yacht to San Diego. But a hurricane turned the dream into a nightmare.

They knew it was going to be a big storm—the weather reports told them that. But Richard and Tami were completely unprepared for what Hurricane Raymond hurled at their sails that October day in 1983. Tami was below checking the barometer when a wave literally plucked the storm-battered yacht from the water… and dropped it from the height of a five-story building. It was more than a day before Tami recovered consciousness. The sea was calm. The sky was blue. But Richard was gone. So were the mast and the radio. When she had recovered from the shock, Tami rigged a tiny sail from the wreckage, and turned the boat toward the nearest downwind island. For Tami, there was no rescue boat, and no spotter plane. She sailed her crippled craft 1,500 mi (2,400 km) all the way to Hilo Harbor, Hawaii.

"I CHECKED THE WIND-SPEED GAUGE AND GASPED WHEN I READ 140 KNOTS."

Two weeks in an ice cave

In 1982 Mark Inglis and Phil Doole were near the top of New Zealand's Mount Cook when a blizzard hit. They were experienced climbers, so they dug a snow cave, climbed in, and waited for the storm to subside.

But the storm didn't let up. Outside what they called their "hotel," 90-mph (145-km/h) winds howled. Inside, the temperature fell to -4°F (-20°C). Over the next five days they shared five biscuits—the only food they had. Their legs turned numb, then froze to ice. On the seventh day, a helicopter dropped supplies. Six days later, they were rescued. It was too late to save their frozen legs, which were amputated (cut off) above the knee. Amazingly this terrible ordeal did not quell their enthusiasm for climbing— Mark went on to climb Everest, becoming the first double-amputee to do so.

Mark Inglis worked with an artificial limb maker to create a range of legs for amputee athletes.

Mega mountain

At 12,316 ft (3,754 m) high, Mount Cook is New Zealand's highest peak. Mark Inglis finally reached the summit 20 years after his ordeal.

Surviving a traumatic climbing experience didn't put double-amputee Mark Inglis off conquering Everest. Here he shows the media his frostbitten fingers upon his return from Kathmandu.

Danger close to home

Aron on the set of *127 Hours*, the 2010 feature film of his accident.

Ours is a crowded, tamed world. Yet, as one hiker found, there is always adventure—and danger— close to home.

Hiking alone in 2003 in Utah, U.S., Aron Ralston moved a boulder. It pinned his right arm to the side of the canyon. After four days, he realized his only chance of escape was to cut off his arm with his blunt pocket-knife. He did it, climbed from the canyon, and was taken to safety by passing tourists.

Lost in the jungle

"I was obsessed with the idea of exploration" says Israeli backpacker Yossi Ghinsberg. But his lust for travel—and gold— almost cost him his life in the tangled rain forest of Bolivia.

Yossi was traveling in South America with two friends when a shady Australian told them of the remote Tuichi River, where gold glitters among the pebbles. The four men set off to find it, but after weeks of jungle trekking, they doubted their guide's skills, and split up. Yossi and an American friend boarded a raft, aiming to float downriver. The river turned to rapids, and the raft to wreckage. Yossi was washed up on a beach, alone. For three weeks he braved sickness, hunger, quicksand, leeches, and jaguars, and had almost given up hope when his friend returned in a motorboat— and ferried him to safety.

Yossi Ghinsberg's guide promised to take them to an unmapped part of the Tuichi River, where the local people guarded "huge chunks of gold" that would make them rich.

Unearth HISTORY

Dig deeper into the mysteries of the past. From ancient artifacts to lost cities, uncover a forgotten world.

◄ Hundreds of terra-cotta soldiers, horses, and chariots were discovered in Shandong, China, in 2002. The soldiers were once painted in bright colors.

ACCIDENTAL Finds

The discovery of an ancient site helps archeologists to uncover the past. Sometimes ordinary people come face to face with history unexpectedly. A farmer may uncover Egyptian pottery, a caver may stumble across Native American arrowheads, or a metal detector may find a hoard of Roman silver. Each piece gives an insight into the history of human life.

THE FACE OF POWER

The Crosby Garrett helmet was found in 2010 in Cumbria, England, using a metal detector. It dates back to between the 1st and 3rd centuries AD. This brass cavalry helmet would never have been practical for the battlefield. It was probably made for the parade ground, or for public ceremonies. The face acted as a visor and the wearer would have struck awe into all who saw him, his face shining like a god.

A SHIP IN MANHATTAN

In 2010, workers building the new World Trade Center in New York City, U.S., uncovered the remains of a wooden ship, with a hull that was 32.2 ft (9.8 m) long. Tests on the wood showed that it dates back to the 1770s, the time of the American Revolution. The sailing ship was a locally built sloop. It had probably traded up and down the Hudson River or along the coast.

SAXON GOLD

In 2009, a metal detector made an incredible discovery—the Staffordshire Hoard. It included more than 3,500 items of gold, silver, and garnets. The artifacts date back to the 7th or 8th century—the time of the kingdom of Mercia. This hoard is the largest collection of Anglo-Saxon gold and silver ever found.

Sacred scrolls

From 1946 to 1947, two shepherds living near the shores of the Dead Sea, Palestine, discovered precious scrolls in some ancient caves. By 1956, they were 972 separate texts had been identified. They were written between 150 BC and AD 70 and include parts of the Hebrew Bible and other writings about religious sects.

A Roman piggy bank

In 2010, a pottery jar was uncovered by metal detecting in Frome, England. It contained 52,503 Roman coins, dating from AD 253–305. Many of the coins were from the time of Carausius, an army commander of Celtic origin who proclaimed himself breakaway Roman emperor in AD 286.

PLANNING A DIG

Archeological digs are carried out by museums, universities, and historical societies. Digs can often last for months. Archeologists and volunteers use special tools so as not to damage any of the finds during excavation.

LEGENDARY Prizes

▶ Schliemann found this stunning gold mask at Mycenae in Greece.

T he greatest archeological finds can change the way we think about the past. Some explorers have devoted many years of their lives to searching for the ultimate sites. Significant discoveries may be in challenging locations, massive in size, incredibly ancient, or even solve a historical puzzle.

Monster move

The big dig—this is the site of Kalhu or Nimrud, in modern Iraq. Here stood the splendid palace of King Ashurnasirpal II, who ruled the Assyrian Empire from 883 to 859 BC. Inside were giant statues of lions and winged bulls with human heads, to guard the king against evil. In 1847 archeologist Austen Henry Layard (1817–1894) decided to move two of these to the British Museum in London, U.K.

Each giant statue weighed about 10 tons. It took 300 men to haul them to the bank of the River Tigris—an epic task!

ALONG WITH THE TERRA-COTTA ARMY, 11 TERRA-COTTA ACROBATS AND STRONGMEN WERE UNCOVERED.

▲ A bearded human head, wearing a sacred headdress, tops the 13-ft- (4-m-) high winged bull statue.

The incredible hunch

Heinrich Schliemann (1822–1890) had always been fascinated by the legends of Greece and Troy. As an archeologist he was an amateur. His methods were wrong and his dating was incorrect—but he was a very lucky man. He located and excavated the ancient site of Troy at Hisarlik, in Turkey. This made people realize that the *Iliad*, an epic poem about the Trojan War, might be based upon events that really took place, thousands of years ago.

Alongside Tutankhamun's coffin, Carter discovered 2,000 treasures.

▶ This dazzling gold mask covered the face of Tutankhamun's mummy.

A glint of gold

The most famous discovery in archeological history began on November 4, 1922, when the archeologist Howard Carter (1874–1939) located a tomb in the Valley of the Kings, in southern Egypt. The valley had been a secret burial ground for Egypt's rulers. The tomb belonged to a young pharaoh called Tutankhamun (c. 1341–1323 BC).

◀▶ The pits containing the life-sized model soldiers were discovered in 1974.

Army of ghosts

In 246 BC, 700,000 workers in Xi'an, China, were given an awesome task—to build a tomb for the first Chinese emperor, Qin Shi Huangdi, and then produce a great army to guard it and protect him in the afterlife. The workers set about creating statues of troops from terra-cotta (baked clay).

◀ In all, there may have been 8,000 model soldiers, 670 horses, and 130 chariots in the burial pits.

MIGHTY Monuments

Throughout history, people have raised massive buildings, monuments, and statues. The builder's aim has been to create a sense of respect, terror, wonder, or delight. For archeologists, they help to show how past societies lived.

Chartres Cathedral

The glorious Rose Window at Chartres Cathedral in France was built around 1215.

TEMPLE OF THE SERPENT

Chichén Itzá in Mexico was a great city of the Maya and Toltec peoples, occupied between the 8th and 13th centuries AD. In its later years, a great stepped pyramid was built there as a temple to the Feathered Serpent god. A snake, carved in stone, adorns the stairways, and twice each year the Sun casts strange snakelike shadows on the northern steps. The monument later became known in Spanish as *el Castillo*, meaning "the Castle."

Chichén Itzá

The pyramid and its platform have one step for each day of the year.

ISLAND GUARDIANS

The first European seafarers to reach the coasts of the remote Pacific island of Rapa Nui ("Easter Island") were mystified by huge stone statues, called Moai. They were carved by the Polynesians who lived there between 1200 and 1680. The tallest statue is 33 ft (10 m) high and the heaviest weighs 86 tons.

EASTER ISLAND MOAI

887 Moai have survived on Easter Island. They represent ancestors who became gods.

Power and praise

Europe's medieval Christian cathedrals were built with massive towers to impress people with the power of God, or with tall spires pointing to the heavens. Inside were golden altars and stained-glass windows to dazzle the eye or to tell picture stories of the saints. These buildings, such as Chartres Cathedral, attracted thousands of pilgrims from across Europe.

MACHINE-AGE MAGIC

Back in 1930, this soaring skyscraper was the world's tallest building. It is still one of the most spectacular sights in New York City, U.S., and a historical landmark. It was originally the headquarters of the giant car manufacturing corporation, Chrysler.

Chrysler Building

This magnificent building has 77 floors and is 1,046 ft (319 m) high.

EVERLASTING LOVE

Its white marble walls are inlaid with gems, its tall towers, or minarets, are graceful and slender, and its domes are reflected in still pools of water. This is the Taj Mahal at Agra, India, and it is believed by many to be the most beautiful building in the world. Constructed between 1630 and 1653, it was built as a tomb to commemorate the love Mughal emperor of India, Shah Jahan, felt for his deceased wife, Mumtaz Mahal. In 1666, Shah Jahan also died and was buried next to his wife.

Taj Mahal

Over 1,000 elephants were used to haul marble to the site.

SECRETS OF STONE

The great pillars of Stonehenge rise from Salisbury Plain in southern England. The stones line up with the positions of the Sun and stars during the year. Stonehenge was probably a site for sacred rituals and was built in several stages between about 2600 and 1600 BC.

STONEHENGE

Some believe that Stonehenge was a calendar, a temple of the Sun, or a center of healing.

ANCIENT Empires

The great empires of the past once wielded immense power, governing vast areas and amassing great wealth. However, with their crumbling monuments all around, we are reminded that no power lasts forever—every empire must fall.

Defending the empire

Power attracts enemies, so empires need strong defenses. The Chinese emperors feared invasion by tribes who lived to the north. Between the 3rd century BC and the 16th century AD they built the world's longest network of fortifications—the Great Wall of China. The wall also served as an east-west route for trade and communications. Although impressive, the Great Wall failed to stop the Mongol invasion of China in the 1200s.

▲ Thousands of miles long, the original wall still stands in places, but some sections have been rebuilt in modern times.

IVORY QUEEN

Great empires often produced awesome works of art. This graceful head represents Queen Idia, the mother of Esigie who ruled the Benin Empire (in modern Nigeria) from 1504 to 1550. Many empires thrived in Africa before their lands were seized by European empire-builders in the 1800s and 1900s.

This ivory mask of Queen Idia is now at the Metropolitan Museum of Art, New York, U.S.

The King of Kings

The ruins of Persepolis still stand in southwest Iran. This was the city of Darius the Great, ruler of the Persian Empire from 522 to 486 BC. Persian lands eventually stretched from Western and Central Asia to Europe and North Africa. It was the biggest empire the world had ever known, ruling about 50 million people.

▼ This bas-relief (projecting image) in Persepolis, Iran, shows people climbing the stairs with offerings for Darius the Great.

DURING THE MING DYNASTY (1368–1644), ONE MILLION SOLDIERS WERE STATIONED ALONG THE GREAT WALL OF CHINA.

Emperor of the Sun

An excited crowd gathers in an ancient Inca fortress at Cuzco, Peru, to watch a spectacular reenactment of the Sun festival of Inti Raymi. In the 1400s and early 1500s, the Inca Empire, called Tawantinsuyu, covered 2,403 mi (3,867 km) of South American coastal strip and mountains. The emperor, or Sapa Inca, was held in awe. He was believed to be a god, descended from the Sun. Each year he made sacrifices at the festival, which was held on June 24 (midwinter in the Southern Hemisphere).

▶ A modern presentation of the ancient Inca festival still impresses the crowds.

Power over peoples

Empires are many lands brought together under a single ruler or government. They depend not only on military power but also on administration, laws, and communications. These skills first came together in the Middle East. The world's very first empire was ruled by the city of Akkad, Mesopotamia, and was founded in 2334 BC by a ruler called Sharrum-Kin or Sargon I. It stretched from the Mediterranean Sea to the Persian Gulf, but had collapsed by about 2160 BC.

◀ This copper head may represent Sargon I, but it is more likely to be his grandson Naram-Sin, who died in 2218 BC.

Code BREAKERS

If we are to travel back in history, we need to know the languages of the distant past. Often the words and scripts are long forgotten. They appear as strange symbols carved on rocks, tombs, or temples. Only language experts can solve these mysteries. Their work may take a lifetime, but if they succeed in cracking the code, they open up a window into the past.

ALLERS
FAMILJ-JOU
Pris: Helår 15: 50.
Allers Familj-Journals tryckeri-aktiebolag, Hälsingborg.
N:r 29.

Just som d... ...ske vetenskapsmannen var i färd med att ...hår när, att han hade

The Rosetta riddle

In 1799 a slab of black stone was found at Rosetta (Rashid) in Egypt. It had been carved in three different scripts in 196 BC to mark the start of a ruler's reign. It was 1824 before all the words on the Rosetta Stone were correctly understood. The code was cracked by French genius Jean-François Champollion.

He started by matching known Greek letters on the third part with the Egyptian symbols on the first part. Then he counted and compared symbol frequency against other texts. The high number of ancient Egyptian hieroglyphs showed that they had to have several functions, representing sounds as well as objects and ideas.

▶ The Rosetta Stone has helped us to understand more about the amazing lives—and the even more amazing deaths—of the ancient Egyptians.

The top part was written in hieroglyphs, symbols that cover ancient Egyptian tombs and statues. No historian could work out what they meant.

The second part was written in Demotic, the everyday language of ancient Egypt. Another mystery.

The third part was written in ancient Greek, which people could understand. Finally, a key had been found to unlock the past.

Sir Henry to the rescue

In the 1830s and 40s, British scholar Sir Henry Rawlinson (1810–1895) became fascinated by carvings on Mount Behistun in Persia (modern Iran). The carvings were written in three ancient languages—Old Persian, Elamite, and Babylonian—and dated from the reign of King Darius the Great (548–486 BC). The inscriptions were written in cuneiform ("wedge-shaped") scripts. Rawlinson and others worked out that the Old Persian script represented sounds. They compared the symbols and their frequency to work out the other two scripts.

◄ Rawlinson risked his life climbing a sheer rockface to get a closer look at the carvings.

History mystery

Great civilizations thrived in the cities of the Indus Valley (modern Pakistan) more than 4,500 years ago. Thousands of objects have been decorated with symbols, but no one knows what they mean. There are few of the repeats and combinations that normally make up a language, but computer tests carried out in 2009 suggest that this really was an ancient script.

► There are said to be about 417 symbols in the Indus script.

IN 2011 A 21-VOLUME AKKADIAN DICTIONARY —MADE UP OF 28,000 CUNEIFORM WORDS—WAS PUBLISHED BY THE UNIVERSITY OF CHICAGO, U.S. IT TOOK 90 YEARS TO COMPLETE AND THE WORK INVOLVED 85 PEOPLE!

Some people believe that the Phaistos Disk is a forgery from 1908.

Back to the future

More than 3,000 years ago, Chinese fortune-tellers carved words onto animal bones and turtle shells, which they threw into a fire. As the bones cracked, the lines that appeared were believed to show glimpses of the future. These "oracle bone" scripts were ancestors of modern Chinese writing and provide historical information about the rulers of that period.

► When farmers dug up these bone fragments, thousands of years after they were carved, they thought they were magical dragon bones.

Secret spirals

The island of Crete, in southern Greece, has many ancient secrets, legends, and ruins. This clay disk was found at the ancient city of Phaistos and dates back to about 1700 BC. Its spirals of stamped designs have never been decoded. Some experts believe that a few of these symbols are similar to a mysterious Cretan script known as Linear A.

Out of the
ASHES

Although ancient people associated volcanic eruptions with angry gods, they often settled nearby because volcanic soil is rich and fertile—it was worth the risk. Volcanoes are symbols of nature's destructive powers, but they sometimes preserve the remains of humans and buildings. These sites are precious time capsules, where a moment in the past is frozen for eternity.

Mega-blast!

One of the most cataclysmic eruptions in history tore apart the Greek island of Thira, or Santorini, near Crete, perhaps in the 1620s BC. The sea rushed in and flooded the vast hole that was left behind. On the surviving land, a town was buried beneath a volcanic stone called pumice. Excavations at this site, named Akrotiri, began in 1967. They revealed drains, furniture, pottery, and stunning paintings in the Minoan style of ancient Crete.

▶ Footprints from the distant past, uncovered by Paul Abell, a member of Mary Leakey's team, in 1978. These hominids not only walked upright, but had feet very like our own.

Fossilized footprints

These footprints at Laetoli in Tanzania look as if they were made only yesterday. In fact, they are about 3.7 million years old and were made long before modern humans had evolved. They belong to hominids, the family of creatures that includes our distant ancestors. The marks were made in fine volcanic ash, which then set hard after being moistened by rain. The footprints became fossilized, preserved forever in stone.

The footprints are 7–8.5 in (18.5–21.5 cm) long.

The remains of Akrotiri reveal how the Minoan people lived more than 3,600 years ago.

Plaster casts capture the moment at which people died in Pompeii.

Plastered!

The Italian city of Pompeii was buried under pumice and ash to a depth of up to 23 ft (7 m). Entire bodies became encased in the ash, leaving imprints as they decayed. Eventually only the skeletons remained. Archeologists discovered that by filling the cavities with plaster, they could recreate the citizens of Pompeii as they had appeared on that fateful day in AD 79.

POMPEII IN A FLASH

Imagine a whole city, stopped in its tracks in AD 79. Half-eaten meals are left on the table, dogs and people cower from the choking ash that showers down relentlessly. The city is entombed. Excavations at Pompeii have revealed the forum (marketplace), temples, streets, shops, houses, gardens, theaters, baths, taverns, laundries, and bakeries.

This carbonized loaf of bread was found in an oven at Pompeii.

This skeleton was excavated from the ruins of Herculaneum, with jeweled gold rings on its finger still intact.

HORRORS IN HERCULANEUM

Herculaneum was a small Italian seaside town just 4 mi (7 km) from Mount Vesuvius. The eruption of Vesuvius in AD 79 blasted it with ash and superhot water, burying the town under 50 ft (15 m) of boiling mud, which turned to rock. Many people fled before the disaster, but 300 or so were stranded in boathouses by the beach, trying to escape. Excavations since the 1700s have uncovered houses, public baths, fountains, jewelry, and wall paintings.

LOST Cities

Can you imagine a modern city such as Sydney, Las Vegas, or Toronto being simply wiped off the map? How might such a site look to an archeologist in the future? Many thriving cities have been destroyed by floods, earthquakes, plague, or warfare. Sometimes climate change has turned fertile lands into deserts, which can no longer provide enough food to feed the city's inhabitants.

▶ Roots and tropical vines partially obscure the stonework of Angkor Wat.

Return of the wild

It takes no time at all for great monuments and cities to be reclaimed by nature. They become eroded by the wind, cracked by frost, or baked by the Sun. Roots and creepers take hold, covering, pushing, and concealing. In Cambodia, the awesome sites of Angkor Thom and the great temple of Angkor Wat, built in the 1100s to 1400s, would be swallowed up by tropical vegetation if they were not constantly cleared and maintained.

▶ Machu Picchu was built in about 1400 and abandoned after the Spanish invasion in 1532.

On the trail of the Incas

On steep mountain slopes in Peru there were mysterious traces of buildings and terraced fields, overgrown with trees and undergrowth. In 1911 an expedition led by the American archeologist Dr. Hiram Bingham (1875–1956) crossed the Urubamba River and climbed up toward the peak of Machu Picchu. Bingham began to clear the ruins and excavate. He discovered finely built stone houses, terraces, steep streets, temples, fountains, and workshops.

Sand and rock

Petra, in Jordan, was once the destination for camel caravans crossing the desert with their riches. The city was set in a cleft of rock and supplied with fresh water by aqueducts. Petra was the capital of the Nabataeans from the 500s BC and came under Roman rule in AD 106. Soon after, trade moved to coastal routes. The West didn't know of Petra's existence until 1812 when it was rediscovered by Johann Ludwig Burckhardt (1784–1817).

▲ Petra's buildings were carved directly from the sandstone rockface.

THE MOAT THAT SURROUNDS THE TEMPLE OF ANGKOR WAT IS 4 MI (6 KM) LONG.

Early life

Çatalhöyük in Turkey was one of the world's earliest towns, settled between about 7500 and 5700 BC. Its houses were joined together, with no streets in between. This was a center of farming, crafts, and religious rituals. It may have been abandoned when trading patterns changed.

◄ This statue of the Mother Goddess was made in Çatalhöyük in about 6000 BC.

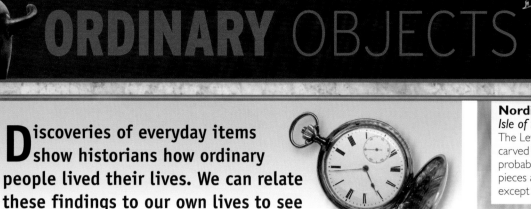

ORDINARY OBJECTS

Discoveries of everyday items show historians how ordinary people lived their lives. We can relate these findings to our own lives to see how things have changed over the years.

Nordic chess piece
Isle of Lewis, Scotland
The Lewis chessmen were carved from walrus ivory, probably in Norway. All the pieces are human shapes, except the pawns.

1300s

Jar for scented oil
Makresia, Greece
Ancient Greeks kept cosmetics, ointments, scents, and oils in ornately decorated terra-cotta containers. Oils made their skin smooth and supple. Rich women also used face powder to achieve a fashionably pale complexion.

1700s

Maori comb
New Zealand
Maori men wore combs carved from whalebone or wood in their topknots (knot of hair arranged on the top of the head). The combs were regarded as sacred possessions.

Greek vase
Greece
Food and wine were stored in terra-cotta containers called amphorae. They kept goods cool.

Early 1900s

Candlestick telephone
U.S.
The first telephones were developed in the 1870s in the U.S. Candlestick phones have a detachable earpiece and standing mouthpiece.

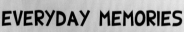

EVERYDAY MEMORIES
The answers to questions about everyday life in the past are revealed by countless little clues. How did people dress and eat? Did they go to school? How did they make a living? How did they communicate with each other?

1900s

Phonograph
U.S.
Also called a gramophone, the phonograph could record and play music.

1400s

Aztec calendar stone
Mexico
This large stone shows details of months and historical ages.

c. AD 600–900
Toy animals
Veracruz, Mexico
The Totonac people of Mexico made ceramic animal figures as toys for their children.

c. 1150

Roman glassware
Rheims, France
Useful glassware was manufactured in many parts of the Roman Empire. These jugs and vases come from ancient Gaul.

c. AD 150

c. AD 1850

Victorian clothes
U.K.
A bonnet, shawl, calico skirt, jacket, and ankle boots were typical working-class clothes in the Victorian era.

5th–6th century

RELIVING THE PAST

Historical reenactments are organized to educate people about the past by making them feel like they are there. Museums and castles often recreate historical scenes by staging displays with actors and actresses. Even schoolchildren can dress up as Romans for the day to get an insight into what life was like in ancient Rome.

1950s

Television
U.S.
The Philco Predicta was a classic set from the early days of television.

50 BC–AD 50

Bronze mirror
Desborough, England
This elegant mirror decorated in the Celtic artistic style dates from Britain's Iron Age.

DRESSING UP

Many schoolchildren get the chance to dress up when they go to visit a museum or a historical building. For just one day they can feel like Victorians, or like a Norman family in a medieval castle.

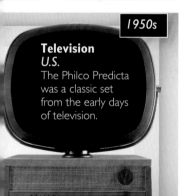

AD 395–632

Wool balls, knitting needle, spool, and spindle
Coptic, Egypt
Ancient Egyptians knitted woolen socks. They had two tubes at the end for their toes, so they could be worn with sandals.

Unearth HISTORY

201

Land of the DEAD

Funeral rituals were already taking place tens of thousands of years ago. The way in which dead bodies have been treated has varied greatly over the ages and among different cultures and religions. The dead person might be buried, cremated, exposed in the open, or preserved as a mummy.

The puzzle of the "Red Lady"

In 1823, a skeleton was found in a cave at Paviland in Wales, U.K., by William Buckland (1784–1856). It was surrounded by shell jewelry and covered in a kind of red ocher. It was immediately assumed that this was the burial of a Roman lady. However, we now know that it was actually a young male who lived just over 29,000 years ago, perhaps the chief of a band of hunters.

▲ The Paviland skeleton is the oldest known ceremonial burial in Western Europe.

▲ A gilded bronze oil lamp in the shape of a kneeling female servant, from the 2nd century BC, was found in the tomb of Princess Dou Wan.

▼ Dou Wan's suit was made up of 2,156 plates of jade.

The eternal princess

In China, princes and princesses were sometimes buried in beautiful suits made of small squares of jade bound by gold wire. This smooth, hard gemstone was believed to be magical, making the wearer immortal and preserving the body. Liu Sheng and his wife, Dou Wan, were buried in about 113 BC. Her tomb contained more than 3,000 precious items.

The grave robbers of Thebes

The trouble with filling the tombs of the dead with fabulous riches is that they attract thieves. To avoid this, the Egyptians began to bury their dead pharaohs in a secret necropolis (burial ground) in the cliffs near the city of Thebes (modern Luxor). Although the "Valley of the Kings," as it became known, was guarded day and night, robbers still managed to break into the tombs and steal the gold.

▲ Grave robbers risked their lives to steal the treasure of the pharaohs.

◄ This statue of a ram from Ur is made of gold, silver, shell, and a blue stone called lapis lazuli.

The royal tombs of Ur

Ur was a city in Mesopotamia (ancient Iraq). Digs in the 1920s revealed 16 royal tombs dating from 2600 to 2500 BC. They were packed with treasure, including golden crowns, gaming boards, a lyre, and exquisite jewelry.

A funeral for a Viking

The Vikings were a seafaring people, so it is not surprising that they often chose to end their days at sea. The bodies of Viking chieftains might be burned in their boats, or gravestones might be laid out in the shape of a boat. This superb longship was found buried under an earthen mound at Oseberg in Norway. It contained the bodies of two women who died in AD 834. One of them may have been a queen.

▼ The Oseberg ship contained dresses, veils, and other textiles, as well as finely carved chests, wooden sleighs, a cart, and the remains of horses, dogs, and an ox.

THE TOMBS OF UR ALSO INCLUDED DEATH PITS, WHERE MANY SERVANTS HAD BEEN SACRIFICED TO ACCOMPANY THE DEAD KINGS AND QUEENS TO THE NEXT WORLD.

Faces of  FOREVER

Some bodies are preserved naturally after death because of the conditions where they are buried. Others have been preserved on purpose for religious reasons, as some cultures believed it would allow the deceased to travel to the afterlife in one piece. The Egyptians perfected this skill.

▼ This mummy from Saqqara was discovered after 2,600 years.

In the land of deserts

Burials in desert sands can dry out dead bodies naturally. This is perhaps how the Egyptians first learned about mummification. They soon developed an elaborate process for preserving corpses artificially, using natron salt, cedar oil, resin, and bandages.

IN THE MIDDLE AGES, MUMMIES FROM RAIDED TOMBS WERE GROUND UP AND USED FOR MAKING MAGICAL POTIONS AND OINTMENTS.

Farewell, Artemidorus

When Egypt came under Greek and then Roman rule, dead bodies were still being mummified and buried in beautiful wooden coffins, which were shaped like human bodies. They were fitted with panels bearing very realistic portraits to provide a reminder of the deceased.

◀ This mummy case from Hawara shows the face of a young man called Artemidorus, who died about 1,900 years ago.

Towers of the dead

Mummification was common in the deserts and mountains of Chile and Peru from 5000 BC until the AD 1400s. In the plateaus of the high Andes, mummies were left in stone towers called chullpas, along with food, drink, knives, pots, and mirrors. In South America, mummies of children were sometimes placed in pottery urns and buried beneath the floor of the family home. Loving parents wanted them to be close at hand, where they could care for their spirit.

◄ This child was mummified during the Nazca period in ancient Peru (c. AD 100–800).

THE EGYPTIANS EVEN MUMMIFIED BABOONS AND CROCODILES!

THE BODIES IN THE BOG

The best-surviving bodies of all have been found in peaty wetlands. In the bogs of northern Europe, the cold, acidic conditions and a lack of oxygen have preserved the skin and organs. The bodies date from about 8000 BC to the early medieval period, but most are from the 5th to 1st century BC. Historians believe that they may have been violently killed as sacrifices to the gods.

▶ A bog man from Lindow Moss, in England. He may have been sacrificed about 2,000 years ago.

Deep frozen

Ice has preserved corpses in the perpetually cold soil of Siberia, and in the mountain glaciers of Europe's Alps—just as if they have been kept in a natural freezer. In 1991 the body of a hunter from Europe's Copper Age was found on the border of Italy and Austria. It had been preserved in a glacier and was given the nickname of Ötzi the Iceman.

◄ The Iceman is the oldest complete human mummy ever to be found. He is so well preserved, even his eyes are still visible.

VISAS   11

Name: Ötzi

Date of birth: c. 3300 BC

Place of Residence: The Alps, Europe

Age at time of death: c. 45 years

Height: 5ft 5 in (1.65 m)

Weight: 110 lb (50 kg)

Distinguishing marks: Tattoos (or needle treatment)

Dress: Bearskin cap, cloak, leather coat, belt, leggings, and shoes

Possessions: Flint knife, bow and arrows, copper ax

HISTORY Lab

Science and technology have transformed the work of historians and archeologists. Special techniques can be used to determine what people ate just before they died, the cause of death, and even what type of work they did. They even reveal what the climate and plant life were like thousands of years ago.

It's all in the trunk

Dendrochronology is the scientific term for counting the annual growth rings in wood. The number of rings offers an accurate year count. The width of the rings provides information about climate and growing conditions.

Genetic tools

DNA is the chemical code of inheritance in all living things and genetics is now a vital tool in archeology. As well as helping to identify a mummy, DNA analysis can also give historians a greater understanding of the time in which the person lived. Diseases the mummy suffered from and medicines it took, as well as its family lineage can also be discovered.

▶ DNA tests suggest that this is the mummy of Hatshepsut, an Egyptian queen who ruled as pharaoh in the 15th century BC.

◀ A sample for carbon dating is taken from a reindeer bone.

Radioactive material

Elements that break down naturally give out radiation. They are said be "radioactive." Organic remains such as wood, grain, textiles, or bones contain both radioactive carbon-14 atoms and stable carbon-12 atoms, which can be compared. The older the object, the less radioactive it will be.

A microscopic triumph

An electron microscope was used to study three tiny grains of pollen found in the stomach of the mummy Ötzi the Iceman. This gave archeologists information about where and when Ötzi died, including the local climate and vegetation, and the season. Electron microscopes were also used to identify food particles in his gut.

▶ Ötzi's last breakfast had been a type of wheat, probably made into a coarse bread.

Call in the dentist

Teeth are the hardest, toughest part of the human body. They often survive long after the bones have rotted away. By studying just one tooth and its wear and tear, it is possible to build up a picture of a person's life. Age, diet, methods of food preparation, general health, stress levels, hygiene, evidence of famine, and lines of descent can all be revealed.

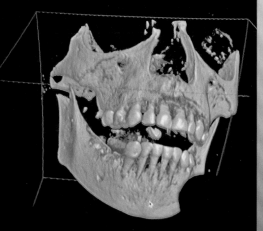

▲ A CT (computer tomography) scan is used to create digital models of a child's jaw and teeth from its 2,000-year-old mummy.

Scans and X-rays

In hospitals, patients can be examined using X-rays and a variety of other scanning technology. This equipment is perfect for examining fragile mummies or other remains. Even removing the delicate bandaging of a mummy can be disastrous, but an X-ray can see straight through to the bone or the skull without causing damage.

▼ This naturally mummified body dates from the 1700s and was taken from a church crypt in Hungary. Scans showed that the cause of death was tuberculosis.

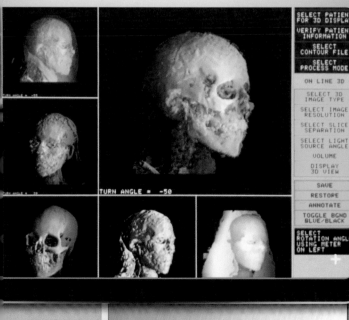

▲ These scans were taken through the closed coffin of an Egyptian temple singer who lived in about 950 BC.

Treasure Trove

Finds of treasure involve fabulous wealth, precious objects, dazzling beauty, and tales of greed and robbery. Valuable discoveries can inform historians about past societies. They learn how things were made and what was considered to be valuable.

HIDDEN HOARDS

Treasure was often hidden in secret places. People may have been smuggling stolen loot, hiding their riches from an invading army, or safely "banking" their money. If the owners were killed or forced to flee before they could reclaim their hoard, its whereabouts may be lost for centuries.

▲ A Viking treasure hoard from about AD 860, found at Hon, in Norway.

▲ The Crusaders shipped the bronze horses back to Venice, Italy, where they became one of the city's most famous sights.

THE SACKING OF A CITY

In 1204, a Christian army of Venetian and French Crusaders bound for the Middle East turned aside to launch a brutal attack on the Christian city of Constantinople (modern Istanbul). They sacked the great churches and palaces, stealing silver, gold, precious stones, pearls, silk textiles, and sacred relics. They carried off a vast fortune and even stole the magnificent statues of horses from the city's racetrack.

FROM THE TOMBS OF LORDS

Many of the most dazzling treasures from all over the world have been found in the tombs and graves of royalty or high-ranking nobles. Grave goods may have been intended as objects for the dead to take to the afterlife, or they may be items of religious ritual or badges of rank.

◀ The Moche "Lord" of Sipán, who lived in Peru about 1,800 years ago, was buried in a pyramid along with gold, silver, and 400 jewels.

CROWN JEWELS

Kings, queens, and emperors liked to display their status and wealth with ceremonial treasures, called regalia, that they wore or carried. Often made of gold or covered in jewels, they included crowns, tiaras, diadems, chains, swords, rings, gloves, orbs (globes), scepters (ornamental staffs), and ermine-trimmed cloaks. Historical crown jewels—or duplicates—are often put on display.

GIFTS FOR THE GODS

People have always made offerings to their spirits or gods, such as incense, sacrifices, or food. "Votive" offerings may also have included fine weapons or jewelry, thrown into a sacred pool or left at a shrine. Medieval rulers would try to win divine favor by giving rich treasures to temples, monasteries, or churches.

◀ The Guarrazar treasure contained crowns, sapphires, and pearls. It was given to the Church in the 600s AD, by Germanic kings who ruled in Spain.

▲ This crown, orb, and scepter were owned by the kings of Poland.

ABOUT 3,000 OF THE OLDEST GOLD ITEMS WERE FOUND IN VARNA, BULGARIA, DATING FROM 4700–4200 BC.

Return to the
BATTLEFIELD

Wartime memorabilia, eyewitness accounts, and historical records help archeologists to build a picture of the realities of wartime. Sometimes their research can reveal forgotten stories, correct inaccurate records, or add significant material to historical archives.

◀ In World War I, the Belgian city of Ypres was destroyed during repeated battles.

French line
Canadian line
British line
Central Division (British)
Cavalry Corps which took the place of the Central Division on May 13
"A" Division (British; originally Colonel Geddes' mixed brigade)

Fading photographs
Traveling back to World War I (1914–1918) is made easier by the widespread use of photography at that time. We can see the expressions on the faces of the young men on both sides as they marched to the front line, lived in the mud of the trenches, and went into battle—history as it actually happened.

▶ Albert "Smiler" Marshall (on horseback) survived World War I and lived until 2005.

Letters and diaries
The authentic voices of World War I soldiers have survived in their diaries and in the letters sent home from the front line, even those that were censored for security reasons by the military authorities.

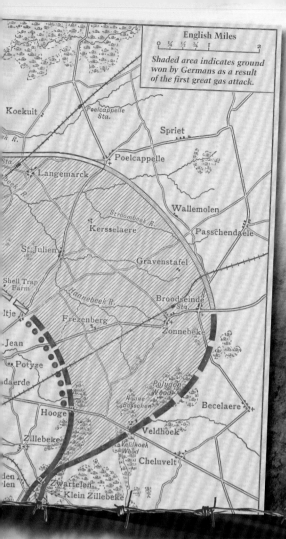

English Miles

Shaded area indicates ground won by Germans as a result of the first great gas attack.

Digging into history

Both sides fighting in World War I (the Allies and the Central Powers) dug networks of trenches to protect their troops, from the North Sea to Switzerland. Archeologists in the Somme region of France dig the battlefield sites to discover the exact position of the trenches of 1916. Archeological finds include skeletons, uniform buttons and badges, helmets, and the remains of weapons, bullets, and shells.

▲ Remains of soldiers who fell during the horrific battles of 1916 are still being uncovered today.

▶ British author Michael Morpurgo visits the Flanders Field Museum in Ypres.

MUSEUMS TELL THE STORY

War was a confusing and terrifying experience for many of the troops on the ground. They could not know the bigger picture of World War I as it progressed. Today, historians can research the tactics and strategies of the generals and the everyday life of the troops by visiting museums and battlefields.

Remembering the soldiers

Cemeteries and memorials are found all over the battlefields of World War I. The huge scale of these burial grounds is a sobering sight. The graves are still visited by descendants of the soldiers who died, and they also provide useful information for war historians.

▲ The names of over 54,000 missing soldiers are recorded on the Menin Gate Memorial in Ypres.

OCEAN Depths

Another world exists beneath the waves. Amid sandbanks and coral reefs, marine archeologists search for the remains of ancient shipwrecks—the victims of storms or naval battles long ago. These are precious time capsules, but are often difficult to access in deep, dangerous waters.

Titanic!

"Titanic" means gigantic, and this was the name given to a state-of-the-art, trans-Atlantic, luxury liner a century ago. In 1912, on its maiden voyage, the ship struck an iceberg and went down with the loss of more than 1,500 lives. It became the most famous shipwreck of all time. In 1985, the remains of *Titanic* were discovered at a depth of nearly 2.5 mi (4 km). More than 6,000 items, including plates and the ship's whistle, have been recovered.

▲ A submersible's camera reveals the rails of the *Titanic*.

Classical cargo

The ancient Greeks were great seafarers and colonists, trading all over the Mediterranean Sea and the Black Sea from the 9th century BC. Wrecks reveal shipbuilding and navigation methods, while surviving cargoes tell us about trading patterns, economics, and even Greek art. Finds include amphorae, the large pottery jars used to store wine and oil.

◀ This is the world's earliest known mechanical computer, dating back to about 100 BC. It was discovered in a Greek shipwreck.

The *Mary Rose* is raised from the seabed in a giant mechanical cradle.

The lost warship

Back in 1545, the warship *Mary Rose* was the pride of the English navy and of King Henry VIII. She was fitted with new "gun ports," openings in the ship's side that allowed the firing of heavy cannon. Sailing out to meet the French fleet, *Mary Rose* flooded and sank. The wreck was found in 1971, many of its timbers preserved under the seabed.

Treasure galleons

After Spanish soldiers invaded Central and South America in the 1500s, they shipped a fortune in looted treasure back to Spain. Between 1566 and 1789, they organized convoys of big sailing ships called galleons to set out from the Caribbean Sea across the Atlantic Ocean. Many ships in these treasure fleets were attacked by pirates, or sunk by hurricanes. The *Nuestra Señora de Atocha* was part of a fleet wrecked on coral reefs off Florida, U.S., in 1622. This ship, with its precious cargo, coins, and cannon, was found in 1985 by American treasure hunters.

▶ This ring and Spanish coin were salvaged from the wreck of a pirate ship, the *Whydah*, which sank off Cape Cod, in North America, in 1717.

IN 1967, DIVERS LOCATED A GREEK CITY THAT SANK BENEATH THE WAVES ABOUT 3,000 YEARS AGO. REMAINS FROM THE PAVLOPETRI SITE HAVE BEEN DATED TO BETWEEN 2800 AND 1200 BC.

Air to GROUND

Archeologists have found the most awesome historical sites—from the air! Images of Earth from air or space can reveal ancient patterns of fields, settlements, or earthworks that could never be seen from the ground. These show the whole of a historic site in its landscape, revealing its overall layout and features.

▼ A microlight aircraft flies over the landscape of Wiltshire in England, which is world famous for its prehistoric monuments.

In the early Middle Ages, Avebury village was built across part of the henge.

High above Avebury

From the ground, the site of Avebury, Wiltshire, U.K., is impressive. From the air, it makes sense. Earthworks form a great ring containing three circles of standing stones. This "henge" was raised from about 2850 BC to 2200 BC, during the New Stone Age. Archeologists believe that it was originally used for ceremonies or rituals.

Stonehenge revealed

The plan of Stonehenge becomes very clear from the air. The position of the great stones and the outer earthworks is emphasized by light and shadow. The site is part of a much larger sacred and ceremonial landscape.

◄ A view never seen during the first 4,900 years of Stonehenge's existence.

Monkey puzzle

Scratched out of the soil in Peru's Nazca Desert are huge patterns and pictures of birds, animals, and people. It was not until the invention of aircraft that people could really see these for what they were. They date back to AD 400–650 and may represent messages to the gods or ceremonial pathways.

SOME OF THE NAZCA DRAWINGS ARE AN ENORMOUS 660 FT (200 M) ACROSS!

▲ This Nazca Desert drawing shows a gigantic monkey with a curly tail.

▶ Found in Ohio, U.S., the first recorded sightings of the Great Serpent Mound are from the 1800s.

Snaking through the landscape

The Great Serpent Mound is the largest animal-shaped mound, or effigy, in the world, at 1,348 ft (411 m) long and up to 3 ft (one meter) high. It is believed to have been built by the Native Americans in AD 1070. After excavating the site, researchers now believe that it was not a burial site.

Rebuilding HISTORY

History can easily be destroyed or lost. Wood rots, stone and brick crumble, costumes deteriorate, written records are easily torn, and precious metals may be stolen and melted down. Saving and recovering the evidence of history is crucial—using conservation, restoration, and reconstruction.

BEFORE

AFTER

▶ Shards of pottery may be carefully reassembled and stuck together.

Jigsaw puzzles

Imagine a vase shattered into a thousand fragments, or an ancient scroll that has disintegrated into a handful of scraps. Often all that remains of a helmet, shield, or bowl are a few crumbling strips of bronze. Experts spend many hours putting together the pieces of the jigsaw, from which pieces may be missing. Sometimes it is not known what the object is until the puzzle is completed.

▼ A painting by Guido Reni (1575–1642) is carefully restored.

BEFORE

AFTER

Canvas and paint

Restoring precious paintings requires painstaking care. Removing centuries of grime or varnish may reveal the colors in startling freshness, or even cast doubt on who painted the picture in the first place. X-rays may reveal corrections the artist has made while painting, or changes that others have made later. Pigments or canvas repairs must be carefully matched with the originals.

BEFORE

BOMB DESTRUCTION

In 1945, as World War II (1939–1945) was drawing to a close, the historical city of Dresden in Germany was razed to the ground by Allied bombing and by a raging firestorm that followed. Decades of reconstruction and restoration began in 1951. The city's great domed church, the Frauenkirche, was completely rebuilt to the exact specifications of the original.

▼ The Frauenkirche lay in ruins after 1945.

AFTER

▼ Reconstruction was completed in 2004–2005.

BEFORE

▼ The temple and statues are cut into blocks of stone, some weighing up to 30 tons each.

AFTER

► The temples are now safe in their new position. This feat was carried out by engineers and archeologists for UNESCO (The United Nations Educational, Scientific, and Cultural Organization).

The Abu Simbel story

Completed in 1224 BC, a great temple complex towered over the Nile valley in southern Egypt. Its twin temples were dedicated to the pharaoh Ramesses II and his wife Nefertari. In the 1950s, a new dam was to be built at Aswan. Unless urgent action was taken, the Abu Simbel site would be flooded by the rising waters of the Nile. From 1963–1968 the entire complex was taken apart, raised to a new, safe position, and rebuilt.

TEMPLES OF TIME

We can't all visit lost cities or discover treasure, but we can go to local historical sites, museums, and galleries. They act as centers of education, research, conservation, and debate. Curators and archivists recreate scenes from the past using real objects and showcase awesome artifacts used by people, hundreds or thousands of years ago.

▶ See the record-breaking American plane *Spirit of St. Louis* (1927) at Washington's National Air and Space Museum.

Get inspired

Designers can get their inspiration from the many fashions of the past. Many museums around the world have stunning displays of historic dress, stage costumes, and fine jewelry.

▲ Fine tapestries from France's National Museum of the Middle Ages, in Paris.

Treasures from around the world

Some of the most famous museums are the Louvre in Paris, France, the Metropolitan Museum of Art in New York City, U.S., the British Museum in London, U.K., and the Smithsonian Museums (19 are located in Washington D.C., U.S.). Exhibits full of historical treasures may be seen from all over the world. Although exciting for visitors, this can be a matter of international dispute as some people believe that treasures should be returned to their homeland.

▲ A ballgown worn by Queen Victoria in 1851 was shown at the Queen's Gallery of Buckingham Palace in London, U.K.

All at sea

Barcelona's medieval royal shipyard is the historic setting for a splendid maritime museum packed with historical ships from ornate galleys to fishing boats. Like many museums it tells you much more besides—about mapping and navigation, political history, trade, and economics.

▼ A replica of the 1568 Royal Galley of Don John of Austria.

Totem poles

Museums of anthropology introduce us to human societies and cultures of the past. This totem pole, made by the Haida people, is from the collection at the University of British Columbia, in Canada. In the 1800s, tall wooden carvings were symbols of power, prestige, and family groups.

◄ Ethnic carvings from long ago still inspire many modern artists and sculptors.

▲ Ancient Babylon's Processional Way (c. 575 BC) is recreated at the Pergamon Museum in Berlin, Germany.

INDEX

Entries in **bold** refer to main subject entries; entries in *italics* refer to illustrations.

ACKNOWLEDGMENTS

The publishers would like to thank the following sources for the use of their photographs:

KEY
AL=Alamy
B=Bridgeman
CO=Corbis
F=Fotolia
FLPA=Frank Lane Picture Agency
GI=Getty Images
IS=istockphoto.com
NPL=Nature Picture Library
PL=Photolibrary
RF=Rex Features
SPL=Science Photo Library
S=Shutterstock
TF=Topfoto

t=top, b=bottom, c=center, l=left, r=right

COVER: 1971yes/S, Ahmad Faizal Yahya/S, Catmando/S, Dmitry Strizhakov/S, Dreamstime, Eric Isselée/S, FABRICE COFFRINI/GI, Germanskydiver/S, Graham Taylor/S, James Laurie/S, Joanne Weston/S, skyhawk/S, Songquan Deng/S, Tatiana Makotra/S, Thomas Zobl/S, Vlad61/S

PRELIMS: 2(c) Le Do/S; 2(c) Ambient Ideas/S; 2–3 avian/S; 2(b) Tinydevil/S; 2(t) Richard Peterson/S; 2(t) Magnolia/S; 3(c) charles taylor/S; 3(b) V.Kuntsman/S; 3(b) topal/S; 3(br) niederhaus.g/S; 3(t) AleksandrN/S; 3(tr) Kamira/S

EARTH'S WONDERS: 4–5 Andrew Aiken/RF; 6–7 Sylvain Grandadam/GI; 6(bl) Image Source/CO; 6(tr) siloto/S; 7(br) TED MEAD/GI; 7(tl) Vakhrushev Pavel/S; 7(tr) David Wall/AL; 8–9 Radius Images/GI; 8(bl) ozoptimist/S; 8(tl) irin-k/S; 8(tr) NASA/CO; 9(br) AR Pictures/S; 9(tr) Gunnar Pippel/S; 9(tl) valdezrl/S; 9(tr) Joel Sartore/S; 9(tr) Steve Collender/S; 10–11 Marc Turcan/S; 10–11 Brian Chase/S; 10(bl) KeystoneUSA-ZUMA/RF; 10(bl) Oxlock/S; 10(bl) Hintau Aliaksei/S; 10(bl) sniegirova mariia/S; 10(tl) nito/S; 10(tl) PILart/S; 11(b) caimacanul/S; 11(b) astudio/S; 11(br) GI; 11(tl) mangostock/S; 12–13 Keattikorn/S; 12–13 exclusive studio/S; 12–13(bc) Ariadne Van Zandbergen/GI; 12–13(tc) Grauvision/S; 12(bl) Lukiyanova Natalia/frenta/S; 12(br) exclusive studio/S; 12(cl) DOELAN Yann/GI; 12(tl) photostudio 7/S; 12(tl) Kompaniets Taras/S; 13(cr) Marilyn Volan/S; 13(br) zimmytws/S; 13(cr) Carolina Biological/Visuals Unlimited/CO; 13(tl) haveseen/S; 13(tr) bonsai/S; 13(tr) Graeme Shannon/S; 14(c) jspix/GI; 14–15 Theo Allofs/CO; 14(bl) Gavriel Jecan/S; 14(bl) Wutthichai/S; 15(cr) Luciano Candisani/Minden Pictures/FLPA; 15(tl) Jurgen & Christine Sohns/FLPA/GI; 16–17 aopsan/S; 16–17 George Steinmetz/SPL; 16(bl) Magnum/F; 16(bl) Cornelia Doerr/GI; 16(bl) magicinfoto/S; 16(br) Tony Waltham/Robert Harding World Imagery/CO; 16(cl) alarik/S; 16(cl) Picsfive/S; 16(tl) Kaspri/S; 17(bc) M.E. Mulder/S; 17(br) AFP/GI; 17(tr) George Steinmetz/SPL; 18–19 José Fuste Raga/GI; 18(tl) ErickN/S; 19(tl) Catherine Karnow/CO; 20–21 Peter Adams/JAI/CO; 20–21(c) Michael Krabs/GI; 20(b) Tadao Yamamoto/amanaimages/CO; 20(b) S; 20(bl) Anan Kaewkhammul/S; 20(tr) R-studio/S; 21(br) Peter Johnson/CO; 21(tr) Charles Bowman/GI; 21(tr) Bomshtein/S; 22–23 Atlantide Phototravel/CO; 22(bl) Ken Welsh/GI; 22(l) Anne Kitzman/S; 22(tr) Vitaly Korovin/S; 23(br) GI; 23(br) Alistair Scott/S; 23(tr) Yvette Cardozo/GI; 24–25 Oliver Lucanus/Minden Pictures/FLPA; 24(bl) ermess/S; 24(cl) Mazzzur/S; 24(tr) Dropu/S; 25(bl) Joanne Weston/S; 25(br) Vlad61/S; 25(br) Merkushev Vasiliy/S; 25(br) yui/S; 25(tr) Reinhard Dirscherl/GI; 25(tr) fotosutra.com/S; 26–27 AF archive/AL; 26–27 Filipchuk Oleg Vasiliovich/S; 26–27 Borodaev/S; 26(br) AF archive/AL; 26(cr) bumihills/S; 27(br) Hemis/AL; 27(br) Tischenko Irina/S; 27(tl) MVaresvuo/GI; 27(tl) S; 27(tr) Eitan Simanor/GI; 28–29 ImageBroker/Imagebroker/FLPA; 28–29(tc) Marina Horvat/ Imagebroker/FLPA; 28(bl) Picsfive/S; 29(br) Georg Knoll/GI; 29(br) Max Topchii/S; 29(tl) Nikki Bidgood/GI; 30–31 PlanetObserver/SPL; 30(t) David Pickford/GI; 31(bl) Pozzo di Borgo Thomas/S; 31(br) Morandi Bruno/GI; 31(tl) Hugh Lansdown/FLPA; 31(tr) ARouse/GI; 32–33(b) Paul Souders/CO; 32–33(t) Barcroft Media/GI; 32–33(t) Roman Krochuk/S; 32(bl) Dr Juerg Alean/SPL; 33(br) Steven Kazlowski/Science Faction/CO; 33(cr) Anthony Cooper/SPL; 34–35 Nejron Photo/S; 34–35 silvae/S; 34–35c Planet Observer/GI; 34(bl) Hefr/S; 34(bl) Hefr/S; 35(bl) Joe Carini/GI; 35(bl) Patrick McFeeley/GI; 35(cr) Yuganov Konstantin/S; 35(tr) Ann Cecil/GI; 36–37 Emmanuel Lattes/AL; 36–37 xpixel/S; 36(bl) Visuals Unlimited, Inc./Reinhard Dirscherl/GI; 36(bl) fotosutra/S; 36(br) Scottchan/S; 36(bl) maxstockphoto/S; 36(l) Malivan_Iuliia/S; 36(t) ronstik/S; 36(t) aboikis/S; 36(tl) HGalina/S; 36(tl) irin-k/S; 36(tl) Scottchan/S; 37(bl) Reinhard Dirscherl/GI; 37(br) inxti/S; 37(tr) Barcroft Media/GI; 37(tr) Steve Collender/S; 38–39 3355m/S; 38–39 PhotoHappiness/S; 38–39(t) Andy Rouse/NPL; 38(bl) Specta/S; 38(br) Mark Conlin/GI; 38(tl) Marilyn Volan/S; 38(tr) Finbarr O'Reilly/ Reuters/CO;

39(b) Stan Osolinski/GI; 39(bl) Seth Resnick/Science Faction/CO; 39(t) Nir Darom/S; 39(tr) George Steinmetz/SPL

AMAZING NATURE: 40–41 Roman Golubenko/Solent/RF; 42–43 Wild Arctic Pictures/S; 42(bl) Joel Blit/S; 42(br) Robert Neumann/S; 42(cr) Sunset/FLPA; 42(l) Sunset/FLPA; 42(l) Jan Martin Will/S; 42(t) Slavolijub Pantelic/S; 43(br) Frans Lanting/FLPA; 43(cl) Rob Reijnen/Minden Pictures/FLPA; 43(t) Doug Allan/GI; 43(t) HABRDA/S; 43(t) Ton Lammerts/S; 44–45 Matthias Breiter/Minden Pictures/FLPA; 44(bl) beboy/S; 44(bl) Darren J. Bradley/S; 44(tl) Picsfive/S; 45(br) Sergey Gorshkov/Minden Pictures/FLPA; 45(l) GI; 45(r) Yva Momatiuk & John Eastcott/Minden Pictures/FLPA; 45(tl) Sergey Gorshkov/Minden Pictures/FLPA; 45(tl) Lukiyanova Natalia/frenta/S; 46–47 Ingo Arndt/Minden Pictures/FLPA; 46–47 Ambient Ideas/S; 46–47 Ingo Arndt/Minden Pictures/FLPA; 46(b) Cathy Keifer/IS; 46(b) Laurie Barr/S; 46(b) jaimaa/S; 46(b) Cathy Keifer/S; 46(cl) robertlamphoto/S; 46(cl) Sari Oneal/S; 46(l) HeinSchlebusch/S; 46(tl) Rtimages/S; 46(tl) Viktorya170377/S; 47(br) Ingo Arndt/Minden Pictures/FLPA; 47(c) Tom Freeze/S; 47(cr) Le Do/S; 48–49 Konrad Wothe/S; 48–49 SVLuma/S; 48(bl) Solvin Zankl/NPL; 48(br) Marcel Jancovic/S; 48(c) Suzanna/S; 48(cr) Jerry Zitterman/S; 48(tl) Doug Perrine/NPL; 49(br) Jeffrey Rotman/CO; 49(br) Ben Jeayes/S; 49(br) Ruslan Nabiyev/S; 49(cl) Hallgerd/S; 49(cl) Benjamin Albiach Galan/S; 49(tl) Matthew W Keefe/S; 49(tr) Visuals Unlimited, Inc./Solvin Zankl/GI; 49(tr) Teeratas/S; 50–51(t) Andy Rouse/NPL; 50(bl) Paul McKenzie/GI; 50(cr) FLPA; 50(tl) SCOTTCHAN/S; 50(tl) irin-k/S; 51(b) Anup Shah/NPL; 51(bl) Iwona Grodzka/S; 51(tl) Zhukov Oleg/S; 51(tl) AridOcean/S; 51(tr) yamix/S; 51(tr) Gentoo Multimedia Ltd/S; 52–53 Doug Perrine/NPL; 52–53(bc) Barcroft Media/GI; 52–53(tc) Barcroft Media/GI; 52(l) funnyboy745/S; 52(tl) MarFot/S; 53(cr) Stuart Westmorland/CO; 53(tl) photo market/S; 53(tr) Doug Perrine/NPL; 54–55 Lorraine Swanson/S; 54(b) Wild Wonders of Europe/Radisic/NPL; 54(b) Matt Jeppson/S; 54(bl) Picsfive/S; 54(t) Rusty Dodson/S; 54(tl) Vasilius/S; 54(tr) Thomas Bethge/S; 55(b) David Thorpe/AL; 55(cr) Mitsuhiko Imamori/Minden Pictures/FLPA; 55(tr) Fedorov Oleksiy/S; 55(tr) rsool/S; 56–57 Yva Momatiuk & John Eastcott/Minden Pictures/FLPA; 56–57(b) James Steidl/S; 56–57(b) max blain/S; 56–57(t) James Steidl/S; 56(bl) Robert Dowling/CO; 56(cl) Jakub Krechowicz/S; 56(tl) Polina Maltseva/S; 57(bl) Roy Mangersnes/NPL; 57(bl) dispcicture/S; 57(br) Jordi Bas Casas/PS; 57(tl) Michael & Patricia Fogden/CO; 57(tr) Mogens Trolle/S; 58–59 Michel & Christine Denis-Huot/GI; 58(bl) mashe/S; 58(l) Nigel Pavitt/JAI/CO; 58(l) Color Symphony/S; 58(tl) Willee Cole/S; 59(bc) Kevin George/S; 59(br) Elliott Neep/FLPA; 59(tr) Image Focus/S; 59(tr) Olga Makhanova/S; 60–61 David Gilder/S; 60–61(bc) Hunor Focze/S; 60–61(bc) Noah Golan/S; 60(bl) Solvin Zankl/Visuals Unlimited/CO; 60(bl) Katrina Brown/S; 60(tl) Michael Durham/Minden Pictures/FLPA; 60(tl) Michael Durham/Minden Pictures/FLPA; 60(tr) Joel Sartore/GI; 61(br) STR/Reuters/CO; 61(br) Eric Isselée/S; 61(tc) Daryl Balfou/GI; 61(tc) Johan Swanepoel/S; 62–63 Ingo Arndt/Minden Pictures/FLPA; 62–63(c) Hiroya Minakuchi/Minden Pictures/FLPA; 62–63(b) Doug Perrine/NPL; 62(c) Georgette Douwma/NPL; 62(c) Augusto Cabral/S; 62(tl) lafoto/S; 63(bl) NatalieJean/S; 63(tr) Sylvain Cordier/GI; 64(c) Roger Powell/NPL; 64–65 Mark Bolton/S; 64(b) Blackbirds/S; 64(cl) Robyn Mackenzie/S; 64(tl) Laborant/S; 64(tr) photocell/S; 65(bl) brandonht/S; 65(br) Gail Johnson/S; 65(br) Bytedust/S; 65(c) shutswis/S; 65(cl) Timothy W. Stone/S; 65(cl) Vitaly Korovin/S; 65(tl) Yuri Shirokov/S; 65(tr) Frans Lanting/FLPA; 66(tl) Olivier Le Moal/S; 66–67 Alena Brozova/S; 66(bl) Frans Lanting/CO; 66(r) RF; 66(tl) Valentin Agapov/S; 67(bl) Brigitte Thomas/GI; 67(br) Pete Oxford/Minden Pictures/FLPA; 67(br) crystalfoto/S; 67(cr) nito/S; 67(tc) Brooke Becker/S; 67(tl) Justine Evans/NPL; 68 (cl) ducu59us/S; 68–69 Feng Yu/S; 68–69 Tungphoto/S; 68(bl) Bruce Davidson/NPL; 68(bl) Brian A Jackson/S; 68(bl) PhotoHappiness/S; 68(br) Hal_P/S; 68(br) Ingvar Bjork/S; 68(cl) Anneka/S; 68(cr) Photo Researchers/FLPA; 68(tr) tanatat/S; 69(c) Kess/S; 69(br) Alex Hyde/NPL; 69(br) Mushakesa/S; 69(cl) GI; 69(cr) Ben Bryant/S; 69(tr) Winfried Wisniewski/FN/ Minden/FLPA; 70–71(tc) Mogens Trolle/S; 70–71 donatas1205/S; 70–71(c) Gavin Parsons/GI; 70–71(t) Barbara Magnuson/Larry Kimball/GI; 70(c) Andy Rouse/NPL; 70(cl) bioraven/S; 70(l) Mazzzur/S; 70(tl) oriori/S; 70(tl) cloki/S; 71(br) Dickie Duckett/FLPA; 71(cr) MarkMirror/S; 71(r) Picsfive/S; 71(tr) Aditya Singh/Imagebroker/FLPA; 72–73 Michio Hoshino/Minden Pictures/FLPA; 72(bl) TungCheung/S; 72(br) Michio Hoshino/Minden Pictures/FLPA; 72(tl) Valentin Agapov/S; 72(tl) kzww/S; 72(tr) morrbyte/S; 73(bl) Dmitriy Bryndin/S; 73(br) Joel Sartore/GI; 73(tl) Rob Crandall/RF; 73(tr) Le Do/S; 74–75 Michael Poliza/GI; 74(bl) Dr. John Michael Fay/GI; 74(bl) Lukiyanova Natalia/frenta/S; 74(cl) 3d brained/S; 74(l) Nihongo/S; 74(tr) Leshik/S; 75(b) Barcroft Media/GI; 75(b) Selena/S; 75(tr) Ulrich Doering/Imagebroker/FLPA

BODY SCIENCE: 76–77 Segalen/Phanie /RF; 79 Cordelia Molloy/SPL; 78–79 aliisik/S; 78–79 Sarunyu_foto/S; 78–79 aopsan/S; 78(tr) Willdidthis/S; 78(tr) R-studio/S; 79(b) Viacheslav A. Zotov/S; 79(bl) vvoe/S; 79(br) Andrea Danti/S; 79(tl) Twelve/S; 79(tl) SeDmi/S; 80 Steve Gschmeissner/SPL; 81 Dr. Kessel & Dr. Kardon/Tissues & Organs/GI; 80(br) SPL/GI; 81(bl) Alexey Khromushin/F; 81(br) J.C. Revy, ISM/SPL; 81(t) Aaron Amat/S; 82–83 Science Picture Co/GI; 82–83 Palsur/S; 82(bl) GRei/S; 82(bl) Linali/S; 84–85 R-studio/S; 84–85(tc) TebNad/S; 84(bl) Michal Kowalski/S; 84(bl) R. Bick, B. Poindexter, Ut Medical School/SPL; 84(br) Litvinenko Anastasia/S; 84(br) Olivier Le Queinec/S; 84(br) B Calkins/S; 84(cl) kedrov/S; 84(cr) Nixx Photography/S; 84(cr) Anusorn P nachol/S; 84(cr) Prof. P. Motta/Dept. of Anatomy/University "La Sapienza", Rome/SPL; 84(tl) Oleksii Natykach/S; 84(tl) ZoneFatal/S; 84(tl) wmedien/S; 84(tl) ojka/S; 84(tr) Yevgen Kotyukh/S; 85(bl) happykanppy/S; 85(br) Anthony DiChello/S; 85(cl) Scimat/SPL; 85(cr) nikkytok/S; 85(tl) Yaraz/S; 85(tl) Steve Gschmeissner/SPL; 85(tr) Volker Steger/SPL; 86–87 Sergey Panteleev/IS; 86(bl) St Bartholomew's Hospital/SPL; 86(br) Paul Gunning/SPL; 86(cr) Fedor Kondratenko/S; 87(br) SPL; 87(t) Dr. Richard Kessel & Dr. Randy Kardon/Tissues & Organs/Visuals Unlimited/CO; 88 Leigh Prather/S; 89 Gunnar Pippel/S; 88(br) Diego Cervo/S; 88(cr) Mikhail/S; 88(cr) Bill Longcore/SPL; 88(l) Scientifica/GI; 88(tr) Ozerina Anna/S; 89(r) Colleen Petch/Newspix/RF; 89(bc) Alex Staroseltsev/S; 89(bl) AFP/GI; 89(bl) Alex Varlakov/IS; 89(br) Martin Dohrn/SPL; 89(cr) Alex011973/S; 89(tl) Eric Gevaert/S; 90–91 Neliyana Kostadinova/S; 90–91 Ramon Andrade 3Dciencia/SPL; 90(br) 3d4medical.com/SPL; 90(l) Sebastian Kaulitzki/S; 90(l) Zephyr/SPL; 91(tr) Sovereign, ISM/SPL; 92–93 Medical Images, Universal Images Group/SPL; 92(bl) Sergey Furtaev/S; 92(cr) Steve Gschmeissner/SPL; 93(bl) Gunnar Pippel/S; 93(br) Kannanimages/S; 93(tl) Similar Images Preview/GI; 94–95 pio3/S; 94–95 Eky Studio/S; 94–95 Mark Beckwith/S; 94(bl) Pascal Goetgheluck/SPL; 94(tr) Suren Manvelyan/RF; 95(br) Anatomical Travelogue/SPL; 95(cl) Ralph C. Eagle, Jr/SPL; 95(cr) Omikron/SPL; 95(tr) guido nardacci/S; 96–97(c) Dragana Gerasimoski/S; 96–97(tc) Carolina Biological Supply Co/Visuals Unlimited, Inc/SPL; 96(bc) Dr Yorgos Nikas/SPL; 96(tl) Medi-Mation/GI; 97(bl) Zephyr/SPL; 97(br) Eugen Shevchenko/S; 97(tr) Simon Fraser/SPL; 98(bc) Monika Wisniewska/S; 98(r) Monkey Business Images/S; 99(r) Troels Graugaard/IS; 99(r) Yuri Arcurs/S; 99(bc) Kais Tolmats/IS; 99(tc) 4x6/IS; 100–101 Franck Boston/S; 100–101(c) Friedrich Saurer/SPL; 100(bl) Thomas Deerinck, NCMIR/SPL; 100(cl) Frederick R. Matzen/S; 100(tr) Aptyp_koK/S; 101(bc) Olga Lipatova/S; 101(br) Professors P.M. Motta, P.M. Andrews, K.R. Porter & J. Vial/SPL; 101(tr) Don Fawcett/SPL; 102–103(c) Gustoimages/GI; 102(bc) SPL/GI; 102(bl) ImageryMajestic/S; 102(cl) Steve Gschmeissner/SPL; 103(br) Netfalls-Remy Musser/S; 103(cl) Gustoimages/GI; 103(tc) Susumu Nishinaga/SPL; 104–105 blackred/IS; 104–105 Skocko/S; 104–105 Angela Harburn/S; 104(bl) Thierry Berrod, Mona Lisa Production/SPL; 104(br) Power and Syred/SPL; 104(t) D. Kucharski & K. Kucharska/S; 104(t) Ultrashock/S; 104(tl) Retrofile/GI; 105(bl) Francis Leroy, Biocosmos/SPL; 105(br) Coneyl Jay/SPL; 105(tr) Dr. Richard Kessel & Dr. Gene Shih, Visuals Unlimited/SPL; 106–107 Ford Photography/S; 106–107 Nata-Lia/S; 106(cl) Andrew Taylor/S; 106(t) Falkiewicz Henryk/S; 106(tl) Igor Kovalchuk/S; 106(tr) Picsfive/S; 106(tr) Johanna Goodyear/S; 107(bl) discpicture/S; 107(tl) Marilyn Volan/S; 108–109 saicle/S; 108(l) Murdoch Ferguson/RF; 109(bl) Mark Carrel/S; 109(bl) Library Of Congress/SPL; 109(br) Dr Yorgos Nikas/SPL; 109(tr) Zephyr/GI; 109(tr) Gordan/S; 109(tr) SAM OGDEN/SPL; 110–111 robertlamphoto/S; 110(bl) kanate/S; 110(c) Sukharevskyy Dmytro (nevodka)/S; 110(cl) Dee Breger/SPL; 110(t) David Mack/SPL; 111(br) Lusoimages/S; 111(br) Michael W. Davidson/SPL; 111(cl) Paul A. Souders/CO; 111(tr) Nils Jorgensen/RF

SPEED MACHINES: 112–113 The World of Sports SC/RF; 114–115(c) David Arts/S; 114(br) Pascal Rossignol/Reuters/CO; 114(tl) AFP/GI; 115–116 kohy/S; 115–116 vlastas/S; 115(b) Bloomberg/GI; 115(c) GI; 115(t) James Leynse/CO; 116–117(c) Travis K. Mendoza/ Navy.mil; 116–117(tc) Richard Vander Meullen/Transtock/CO; 116(bl) Olga Gabay/S; 117(br) Pascal Rossignol/Reuters/CO; 117(t) Karl R. Martin/S; 118–119 Evgeny Karandaev/S; 118–119(c) The Boeing Company/Wright-Patterson Air Force Base; 118(bc) ra2 studio/S; 118(bl) NASA-DFRC; 119(bl) Reaction Engines Ltd; 119(bl) ra2 studio/S; 119(tr) NASA-DFRC; 119(tr) cifotart/S; 120(c) Graham Bloomfield/S; 120–121(bc) GI; 120(bl) Josh Cassatt/Navy.mil; 120(bl) rodho/S; 121(br) Dennis MacDonald/AL; 121(br) Stillfx/S; 121(t) GI; 120–121 Eliks/S; 122(cl) SSPL/GI; 122(cl) Karl R. Martin/S; 122(l) Valerie Potapova/S; 123(cl) David Ducros/SPL; 123(cr) AFP/GI; 123(t) Friedrich Saurer/SPL; 124–125 AFP/GI; 124–125 caimacanul/S; 124(l) Ventura/S; 124(t) Helena Darvelid/Vestas Sailrocket; 124(t) Alhovik/S; 125(b) Gamma-Rapho/GI; 125(tl) Ingrid Abery/ActionPlus/TF; 126–127 GI; 127(r) Powerboat P1; 127(tl) Ilene MacDonald/AL; 128–129 Sipa Press/RF; 128–129 Eky Studio/S; 128(l) Canadian Press/RF; 129(r) GI; 130–131(c) Hank Morgan/SPL; 130(bl) CO; 130(c) Linali/S; 130(t) Antony Nettle/AL; 131(br) frank'n'focus/AL; 131(tr) Louie Psihoyos/CO; 132–133 Vladitto/S; 132–133(t) GrandeDuc/S; 132(bl) Bruce Frisch/SPL; 132(tl) Stephen Morrison/epa/CO; 133(bl) doodle/S; 133(br) Schlegelmilch/CO; 134–135 Allgusak/S; 134–135 grynold/S; 134–135 silvae/S; 134–135(b) VikaSuh/S; 134–135(ct) andkuch/S; 134–135(tc) Max Earey/S; 134(cl) Stuart Elflett/S; 134(cr) Naiyyer/S; 134(tl) Callahan/S; 135(cl) testing/S; 135(cr) minik/S; 136–137 sootra/S; 136–137 Kitch Bain/S; 136(bc) mobil11/S; 136(bl) AMA/S; 136(bl) Neo Edmund/S; 136(br) Ahmad Faizal Yahya/S; 136(cl) titelio/S; 136(tl) LongQuattro/S; 136(tr) Tom Hirtreiter/S; 137(bc) Sergei Bachlakov/S; 137(bl) Kitch Bain/S; 137(bl) Darren Brode/S; 137(tc) manzrussali/S; 137(tl) aditya katyal/AL; 137(tl) Christopher Halloran/S; 137(tr) Gabriella Ciliberti/S; 138–139 yexelA/S; 138–139(c) Smithsonian Institution/CO; 138(bl) Boeing/Joe Olmos/NASA; 138(bl) spaxiax/S; 138(tl) Luc Sesselle/S; 139(b) oneo/S; 139(br) Jim Amos/SPL; 139(tr) Elnur/S; 139(tr) Apostrophe/S; 139(tr) Detlev Van Rvenswaay/SPL; 140–141(c) GI; 140(bl) Barcroft Media/GI; 141(r) Roman Sotola/S; 141(bl) Tony Watson/AL; 141(r) NASA/SPL; 141(tl) Leo Mason/CO; 142 P. WALLICK/ClassicStock/TF; 142–143(b) Charles M. Ommanney/RF; 142(tl) jelome/S; 143(br) Topham/UPP/TF; 143(tr) Trinity Mirror/Mirrorpix/AL; 144–145 avian/S; 144–145 agsandrew/S; 144(bl) A3250 Oliver Berg/dpa/CO; 146–147 Goran Bogicevic/S; 146(br) Christian Darkin/SPL; 146(c) Deco/AL; 146(c) R-studio/S; 146(t) RF; 147(br) Simon Holdcroft/AL; 147(cl) Sikorsky/RF; 147(t) NASA

THRILL SEEKERS: 148–149 Unimedia Images/RF; 150 GI; 150–151 Werner Muenzker/RF; 150(br) Daniel Ramsbott/dpa/CO; 151(br) Roger-Viollet/RF; 151(c) Unimedia Images/RF; 151(t) Deymos/S; 152–153 Thomas Zobl/S; 152(b) Kesu/S; 152(bl) GI; 153(br) Petrosg; 153(c) Sam Tinson/RF; 153(c) Cre8tive Images/S; 153(tl) Ulza/S; 153(tr) Christopher Groenhout/GI; 154 Wronaavd/S; 154(r) Kokhanchikov/S; 154(cr) Martin Lehmann/S; 154(tc) Martin Lehmann/S; 154(tl) Martin Lehmann/S; 155(c) fuyu liu/S; 155(bl) GI; 155(br) National Geographic Image Collection/AL; 155(t) Sports Illustrated/GI; 156–157 Nicemonkey/S; 156(bl) National Geographic/Everett/RF; 156(br) Marcel Jancovic/S; 156(t) A Cotton Photo/S; 157(b) Hugh Sitton/CO; 157(t) Amy Toensing/GI; 157(tl) Alfredo Dagli Orti/The Art Archive/CO; 158–159 maga/S; 158(br) Tyler Stableford/GI; 158(l) GI; 159(bc) Â©ullsteinbild/TF; 159(bl) Jakub Krechowicz/S; 159(br) Morphart/S; 159(tl) Vitaly Korovin/S; 159(tl) The Granger Collection?TF; 159(tr) GI; 160–161 Losevsky Pavel/S; 160–161(c) Steve Maisey/RF; 160(bl) Hulton-Deutsch Collection/CORBIS; 160(bl) Christophe Boisson/S; 160(cl) Lightspring/S; 160(tl) bepsy/S; 160(tl) Christophe Boisson/S; 160(tr) Perov Stanislav/S; 161(br) Bongarts/GI; 161(t) AFP/GI; 162–163 Mikhail Nekrasov/S; 162–163 NitroCephal/S; 162–163(b) Nino Cavalier/S; 162–163(b) Kellis/S; 162(bl) Mariana Bazo/X00023/Reuters/CO; 162(bl) Sergey Mironov/S; 162(br/tr) Chayne Hultgren (www.thespacecowboy.com); 162(c) Ton Lammerts/S; 163(br) Sipa Press/RF; 163(tc) DJTaylor/S; 163(tl) KeystoneUSA-ZUMA/RF; 163(tr) Kacso Sandor/S; 164(b) Jack Dempsey/AP/PAI; 164(b) ajt/S; 164(tr) Alfredo Escobar/epa/CO; 165(c) Nils Z/S; 165(b) John D McHugh/AFP/GI; 165(cl) Alexis Rosenfeld/SPL; 165(t) Bettmann/CO; 166–167(tc) Steve Marcus/Reuters/CO; 166(b) William West/AFP/GI; 166(b) saiko3p/S; 167(b) Paul Roberts/Offside/CO; 167(bc) patrimonio designs limited/S; 167(t) GI; 167(tc) Ian O'Hanlon/S; 168 Fedorov Oleksiy/S; 168–169 National Geographic/GI; 168–169 swinner/S; 168–169(b) Mark S. Cosslett/GI; 168(t) National Geographic/GI; 169(b) Barcroft Media/GI; 169(t) Stephen Alvarez/GI; 170(br) Benoit Stichelbaut/bluegreenpictures.com/RF; 170(c) Mary Evans Picture Library/AL; 170(tl) marekuliasz/S; 171(br) Charles Platiau/Reuters/CO; 171(tl) RF; 171(tr) Sipa Press/RF; 172–173 Action Press/RF; 172(bl) Gamma-Rapho/GI; 173(r) WireImage/GI; 173(r) Maria Toutoudaki/IS; 173(bl) Rick Doyle/CO; 173(tl) Agencia EFE/RF; 173(tl) Anan Kaewkhammul/S; 174 Tim Clayton/CO; 174–175(b) Maygutyak/F; 174(b) Peter Klaunzer/epa/CO; 174(tl) shutswis/S; 175(cr) MountainHardcore/S; 175(r) Aurora Photos/AL; 175(t) Ross Woodhall/GI; 175(tl) Walter Quirtmair/S; 176–177 Rob Howarth/RF; 176(cl) Bettmann/CO; 177(br) Tyler Stableford/GI; 177(tl) Swim Ink 2, LLC/CO; 177(tr) GI Sport; 178–179 Sam Cornwell/S; 178–179(c) taboga/S; 178–179(t) Claudio Santana/AFP/GI; 178–179(tc) Creatista/S; 178(bl) Brooke Whatnall/S; 178(l) DGDesign/S; 178(l) Poprugin Aleksey/S; 179(bl) 808isgreat/S; 179(br) GI; 179(r) Arne Dedert/epa/CO; 180–181 Ljupco Smokovski/S; 180–181 benchart/S; 180–181 Christophe Boisson/S; 180(br) William West/AFP/GI; 180(c) Popperfoto/GI; 180(tr) Ken McKay/RF; 181(br) GI; 181(tr) Starstock/PS; 182(r) F; 182–183 charles taylor/S; 182–183 Dr. Morley Read/S; 182(bc) c.IFC Films/Everett/RF; 182(br) Taiga/S; 182(l) c.IFC Films/Everett/RF; 182(tr) airn/S; 183(bl) migin/IS; 183(bl) Gemenacom/S; 183(br) f9photos/S; 183(br) Michael C. Gray/S; 183(cr) Face to Face/PS; 183(cr) FoxSearch/Everett/RF; 183(tl) AP/PAI; 183(tr) GI

UNEARTH HISTORY: 184–185 Mark Campbell/RF; 186–187 Lanica Klein/GI; 186–187 val lawless/S; 186–187(b) Eddie Keogh/Reuters/CO; 186(cl) GI; 186(tl) Sergey Kamshylin/S; 186(tr) Sipa Press/RF; 187(br) Kirsanov/S; 187(c) Nils Jorgensen/RF; 187(c) Hintau Aliaksei/S; 187(c) Leigh Prather/S; 187(tr) West Semitic Research/Dead Sea Scrolls Foundation/CO; 188–189 mack2happy/S; 188–189 sniegirova mariia/S; 188–189(bc) Eastimages/S; 188(bl) Selyutina Olga/S; 188(br) Jon Bower London/AL; 188(cl) Cameramannz/S; 188(cl) Valentin Agapov/S; 188(cr) GI; 188(l) Ultrashock/S; 188(tl) nulinukas/S; 189(br) GI; 189(c) val lawless/S; 189(cl) GI; 189(tr) Brian Rasic/RF; 189(tr) BW Folsom/S; 190–191 Cristina Ciochina/S; 190–191(bc) gary yim/S; 190–191(tc) St. Nick/S; 190(bl) Manda Nicholls/S; 190(bl) ChaosMaker/S; 190(cl) Amenhotepov/S; 191(b) Phase4Photography/S; 191(c) Igor Plotnikov/S; 191(cr) Yuri Yavnik/S; 191(r) SeanPavonePhoto/S; 191(tr) 100ker/S; 192–193 Ed Lemery/S; 192(bl) Werner Forman/CO; 192(t) Eky Studio/S; 192(tc) John Lock/S; 192(tl) Wuttichok/S; 193(r) mrfotos/S; 193(bl) Time & Life Pictures/GI; 193(cr) Keren Su/China Span/AL; 193(tr) Joel Blit/S; 194–195(t) Mary Evans Picture Library/AL; 194(bc) Kapu/S; 194(bc) Hintau Aliaksei/S; 194(bl) Pokaz/S; 194(cr) grintan/S; 194(r) Dea Picture Library/GI; 194(tl) Mark Carrel/S; 195(bc) The Art Gallery Collection/AL; 195(bl) Jill Battaglia/S; 195(bl) Valentin Agapov/S; 195(br) Jakub Krechowicz/S; 195(cl) Sergey Peterman/S; 195(r) Gianni Dagli Orti/CO; 195(tl) Leigh Prather/S; 195(tr) Charles & Josette Lenars/CO; 195(tr) Valentin Agapov/S; 195(tr) Kenneth V. Pilon/S; 196–197 Mark Yarchoan/S; 196–197(t) De Agostini/GI; 196(br) Kenneth Garrett/National Geographic Stock/GI; 196(br) Hefr/S; 196(tl) Anan Kaewkhammul/S; 196(tl) Anan Kaewkhammul/S; 197(bl) Nattika/S; 197(br) Jonathan Blair/CO; 197(c) Anan Kaewkhammul/S; 197(cl) Spectrum Colour Library/HIP/TF; 197(cr) Ulza/S; 197(t) TF; 198–199 Pavol Kmeto/S; 198–199(b) Jarno Gonzalez Zarraonandia/S; 198(bl) David Davis/S; 198(cl) Sergej Razvodovskij/S; 198(t) Steve Collender/S; 198(tl) HGalina/S; 198(tl) Danny Smythe/S; 198(tl) Khoroshunova Olga/S; 199(b) Nathan Benn/AL; 199(br) rodho/S; 199(cr) vittorio sciosia/AL; 199(tr) nito/S; 200–201 avian/S; 200–201(t) Time & Life Pictures/GI; 200(bl) Toni Dal Lago/S; 200(bl) Dja65/S; 200(bl) Yuri Shirokov/S; 200(br) Artem Mazunov/S; 200(br) niederhaus.g/S; 200(cl) Holly Kuchera/S; 200(tl) liubomir/S; 200(tl) TF; 200(tr) Werner Forman/CO; 200(tr) Evgeny Murtola/S; 201(r) Dorling Kindersley/GI; 201(bc) prism68/S; 201(bl) Luisa Ricciarini/TF; 201(c) Werner Forman/CO; 201(cl) Kamira/S; 201(cl) Kamira/S; 201(t) The Granger Collection/TF; 201(tc) Persian School/GI; 202–203 thepiwko/S; 202–203(b) Asian Art & Archaeology, Inc./CO; 202(b) Lucy Baldwin/S; 202(bc) silky/S; 202(cr) Paul D Stewart/SPL; 202(tr) Traci Law/S; 203(cr) altrendo travel/GI; 203(l) CO; 203(tr) Eugene Sergeev/S; 203(tr) italianestro/S; 204–205 Julio Donoso/Sygma/CO; 204(bl) The Granger Collection/TF; 204(tr) AFP/GI; 205(bl) Copper Age/GI; 205(br) blinow61/S; 205(br) Patrick Landmann/SPL; 205(cr) for you design/S; 205(tr) TF; 205(bl) ivn3da/S; 206(bl) James King-Holmes/SPL; 206(c) WpN/PS; 206(tl) J. Helgason/S; 207(bl) martiin fluidworkshop/S; 207(bl) Alexander Tsiaras/SPL; 207(br) ullsteinbild/TF; 207(cl) R-studio/S; 207(tr) Michael Maloney/San Francisco Chronicle/CO; 207(tr) Linali/S; 208–209 nav/S; 208–209 nav/S; 208(b) R-studio/S; 208(bl) Mimmo Jodice/CO; 208(cr) Giraudon/B; 208(l) Vladislav Gurfinkel/S; 208(tl) Kompaniets Taras/S; 208(tl) Neo Edmund/S; 208(tr) Nathan Benn/AL; 209(br) Sergios/S; 209(l) zhu difeng/S; 209(t) idea for life/S; 209(tr) bilwissedition Ltd. & Co. KG/AL; 210 Bettmann/CO; 210(c) Lou Oates/S; 210–211 Ladyann/S; 210–211(t) Classic Image/AL; 210(b) Jakub Krechowicz/S; 210(bc) Mike Hollist/Daily Mail/RF; 210(bl) Richard Cano/IS; 210(cl) frescomovie/S; 211(b) Brian Harris/RF; 211(cl) Brian Harris/RF; 211(tr) GI; 212–213 Borut Furlan/PL; 212–213 fuyu liu/S; 212(bl) Ancient Art & Architecture Collection Ltd/AL; 212(cl) Emory Kristof/National Geographic Stock/GI; 213(br) Richard T. Nowitz/CO; 213(br) Steve Collender/S; 213(t) Nils Jorgensen/RF; 214– 215 Flyfoto/AL; 214–215 agap/S; 214(bl) Last Refuge/Robert Harding World Imagery/CO; 215(br) Mark Burnett/AL; 215(tr) Maria Toutoudaki/IS; 215(tr) Tomas Kunzt/S; 216 Anelina/S; 216(cl) V. Kuntsman/S; 216(bl) Phil Yeomans/RF; 216(bl) Iaroslav Neliubov/S; 216(br) pzAxe/S; 216(br) Laborant/S; 216(tl) Excellent backgrounds/S; 216(tr) Gamma-Rapho/GI; 217(bl) AFP/GI; 217(br) Paul Vinten/S; 217(cr) topal/S; 217(t) Charles Taylor/S; 217(tl) ullsteinbild/TF; 217(tr) Nata Sdobnikova/S; 218–219 pio3/S; 218(tr) B Christopher/AL; 218(br) PA Photos/TF; 218(cl) imagelab/GI; 218(cl) Shevchenko Nataliya/S; 218(t) Ampirion/S; 219(b) Spectrum/HIP/TF; 219(bl) All Canada Photos/AL; 219(br) Illman/S; 219(tr) Jean-Pierre Lescourret/CO

All other photographs are from:
Corel, digitalSTOCK, digitalvision, Dreamstime.com, Fotolia.com, iStockphoto.com, John Foxx, PhotoAlto, PhotoDisc, PhotoEssentials, PhotoPro, Stockbyte

Every effort has been made to acknowledge the source and copyright holder of each picture. The publishers apologise for any unintentional errors or omissions.